MORE THAN MEETS THE EYE

ENCOUNTERING GOD WHERE WE LEAST EXPECT TO FIND HIM

DENNIS E. HENSLEY

Kregel
Publications

More Than Meets the Eye: Encountering God Where We Least Expect to Find Him

© 2004 by Dennis E. Hensley

Published by Kregel Publications, a division of Kregel, Inc., P.O. Box 2607, Grand Rapids, MI 49501.

Cover design: John M. Lucas

ISBN 0-8254-2792-4

Printed in the United States of America

04 05 06 07 08 / 5 4 3 2

This book is joyfully dedicated to
my longtime dear friend and Christian brother,
Steve Summers,
a man who has at various times been my
business partner, my associate on deacon boards and
school boards, and at all times my
confidant and pal.
Everyone should have
one friend this great.

CONTENTS

ACKNOWLEDGMENTS

I wish to thank my daughter, Jeanette, who worked diligently as my secretary during the preparation of this book. Others who have been friends and encouragers at various times in my life include David and Nancy Gyertson, Jim Roznowski, Ron Sloan, Jay Kesler, Steve and Lucia Resch, Pam Jordan, Daryl Yost, Neil Ringle, Tom Beckner, Lin Johnson, Steve Barclift, Jack Williams, Marlene Chase, Doug Barcalow, Bob and Julia Baker, Michael Landon Jr., Holly G. Miller, Jay Platte, Bill Myers, Jim and Ann Holmes; my parents, Ed and Juanita Hensley; my sister, Pam; my wife, Rose; my brother, Gary, and his wife, Donna; my son, Nathan; and my childhood Sunday school teacher, Al Sprague.

CHAPTER 1

AN ACT OF GOD

Three days after I gave a motivational speech to a large crowd of business executives, I received a phone call from a woman who was the chief financial officer of her corporation.

"I was captivated by your optimistic outlook on life and your entertaining sense of humor," she told me. "Our company—and particularly our accounting and finance department—needs a dose of that. Can you come by my office to discuss some bookings?"

The next afternoon I was seated in front of her desk, telling her about my workshops and seminars. Suddenly, in the midst of my presentation, she interrupted me.

"This isn't it," she said bluntly.

I paused, looking at her quizzically.

She waved her hands. "I'm sure these programs of yours are excellent," she explained, "and we'll probably have you do one or two for our people. But this . . . this 'training' isn't what I want personally. What *I* want is to become like *you*. I want the optimism and happiness you have. I want you to be my role model."

I shook my head. "I'm flattered," I said, "but I'm the wrong choice. I'm as prone to failure and poor judgment as anyone else."

She seemed terribly disappointed by my candor.

"However," I continued, "I can point to Someone who *is* worthy of patterning your life after. He never fails at anything and His judgment is always perfect. In fact, what you envy about me comes from my relationship with this Person. And you can develop that same relationship."

I pulled a tract from my briefcase and spent the next ten minutes sharing the message of salvation with her. She seemed genuinely interested, although not totally convinced that this was what she needed.

"I've given some thought to religion," she said at last, "but I guess I've always found it hard to believe that God really exists. I'm a very pragmatic person. I deal in cost factors, work hours, contracts, insurance . . . things that can be determined in black and white."

I weighed that a moment, then asked, "Do you oversee the insurance coverage of this building for fire, vandalism, and the like?"

"Yes," she said, "that comes under my department. Why?"

"Get the policy, will you?"

She hesitated, but then left the office and came back with the paperwork. She handed it to me and I flipped through the pages. I found what I was looking for and pointed to a paragraph.

"According to this section of the policy," I said, "you are covered for 'acts of God.' What are those?"

She grinned. "You know," she said, shrugging her shoulders. "An 'act of God' is something we have no control over. Like if lightning strikes our building or the river floods us out or a hurricane blows in. Things like that."

"And do you believe that's possible?" I asked. "Could an 'act of God' really occur?"

"Sure it could," she insisted. "You live around here. You remember the tornado that came through this very area last spring. It knocked a dozen buildings flat just eight blocks from here."

"That's true," I said. "So, then, you feel that the $3,000 your company pays each year to insure this entire building is worth the money?"

"I'm not saying we *enjoy* spending that money," she admitted, "but one 'act of God' without insurance and we would be in a hopeless situation. It just helps us all breathe easier knowing that we're covered in case something ever happened."

"Exactly!" I said. "And that's the difference between you and me. That's the element of life that I have but you're missing. It's what you see in me that you can't define but you know you want."

"What?" she said, almost chuckling. "An insurance policy?"

"Yes, an insurance policy," I responded seriously. "One day there is going to be 'an act of God' in your own life. You're going to die. There's no avoiding it, and you know it's true. It could be today or next year or several decades from now. In time, however, it *will* happen. I've accepted Christ as my Savior and He's assured me of a home in heaven with Him for all eternity. So, I don't dread that forthcoming 'act of God' in my life. But you . . ."

She stared at me.

"You're saying I'm walking around uninsured," she said, finishing my thought. "You're telling me that I can't breathe easy because in the back of my mind I know that, if something should ever happen to me, I'll be in a hopeless situation."

"Yes," I confirmed, "that's it. I believe that's why you really asked me to your office today. You needed to find out what was missing in your life. And now you know."

The room went silent for a moment, and the woman sat looking at her folded hands in her lap.

After a time, I asked, "So, how about it?"

"W-what?" she said, lifting her eyes.

"Are you interested in getting an insurance policy?" I asked. "The premiums are free and the dividends are immeasurable. Best of all, one policy gives you coverage for all 'acts of God.' Would you like one?"

She let out a long breath of air, smiled slowly, then said softly, "Yes. Let's go over this tract once again. I want to see how I can get a lifelong policy."

SCRIPTURE VERSES TO PONDER

In the beginning God created the heavens and the earth. Now the earth was formless and empty, darkness was over the surface of the deep, and the Spirit of God was hovering over the waters. And God said, "Let there be light," and there was light. God saw that the light was good, and he separated the light from the darkness. God called the light "day," and the darkness he called "night." And there was evening, and there was morning—the first day.

—Genesis 1:1–5

Then Jesus directed them to have all the people sit down in groups on the green grass. So they sat down in groups of hundreds and fifties. Taking the five loaves and the two fish and looking up to heaven, he gave thanks and broke the loaves. Then he gave them to his disciples to set before the people. He also divided the two fish among them all. They all ate and were satisfied, and the disciples picked up twelve basketfuls of broken pieces of bread and fish. The number of the men who had eaten was five thousand.

—Mark 6:39–44

QUESTIONS TO CONSIDER

1. In his quest to explain the phenomena of nature without giving credit or praise to God, sinful man has created everything from false gods to false science. In what ways do you think such things as humanism, evolution, and other unbiblical teachings are impacting our world today? What can we do to present an opposing view and to share our message of God's creationism?
2. How many great "acts of God" can you recall from the Old and New Testaments? In what ways did God use the great flood, the

parting of the Red Sea, the forming of the Bethlehem star, and other great miracles to proclaim His deity?

3. Despite the fact that Jesus performed such "acts of God" as walking on water, raising the dead, healing the sick, feeding the hungry, and forgiving the sinful, He was rejected and scorned. Why do you think the heart of man finds it so difficult to accept the claim of Christ that He and the Father are One?

SUGGESTED ADDITIONAL READING

Jones, Peter. *Pagans in the Pews.* Detroit: Regal, 2002.

Rima, Samuel D. *Leading from the Inside Out: The Art of Self-Leadership.* Grand Rapids: Baker, 2000.

Sjogren, Steve. *Conspiracy of Kindness: A Refreshing New Approach to Sharing the Love of Jesus with Others.* Ann Arbor: Vine Books, 1993.

Strohmer, Charles. *The Gospel and the New Spirituality.* Nashville: Nelson, 1996.

CHAPTER 2

ONLY BLOOD SAVES LIVES

We were all poor, so it didn't matter.

I was halfway through my studies for a Ph.D. in English. My wife and I were "existing" on my G.I. Bill education benefits and a small stipend I received for teaching freshman composition courses. Our used car was rusty, our clothes weren't new, and our "dates" consisted of cheese and crackers in front of an eighteen-inch black and white television.

But we weren't alone. The other doctoral candidates were also young marrieds, some with small children. They were scraping by, like us, in hopes of completing a Ph.D. and then landing a plum position teaching literature at a prestigious university—big salary, nice office, full benefits package.

In the meantime, life was sparse. Tuition, books, and research costs absorbed most of our earnings. I was sharing a cramped office with a fellow named Dave Haire. Whenever a semester would end and we would do well on our grades, Dave and his wife, Ann, and my wife, Rose, and I would get together with other couples to celebrate. These "celebrations" consisted of grilled hot dogs, potato chips, and Kool-Aid. Like I said, we were all poor.

But the times were great anyway. We'd sit around and talk about books and authors, about the classes we were taking and the ones we were teaching, and, of course, about the day when we'd finally graduate and become professors.

During this second year of doctoral studies, my wife gave birth to our first child. Because of a bout with anemia, Rose had been given iron shots during her pregnancy; however, the trauma of the birth had caused her to lose a lot of blood and had depleted her strength. To help her recover, the doctors had given her numerous transfusions.

Although my insurance covered 80 percent of the delivery costs, I still had a lot of bills to pay. On top of all that, there was a new bill for $380 for the extra pints of blood my wife had required. I had no idea how I was going to get the money to pay for the blood.

"Lord, I need a miracle," I prayed. "I'm broke and worried and overworked. I need You to get me through this crisis."

My office partner, Dave, called to check on things.

"You don't have $380 you could loan me, do you?" I asked, as I explained about the bill for the transfusions.

"I don't even have $3.80 to loan you," he admitted. "But I'll ask the other doctoral candidates. Maybe we can raise *something* if we pool our nickels and dimes."

I fretted all that afternoon and all that night, knowing that when I went to see my wife and baby the next day I would also have to go by the hospital's accounting office to discuss the bill.

The next morning as I entered the hospital, I decided to tackle my financial problem before going to see my wife. I determined that I'd just have to tell the hospital accountant I was broke and that I'd have to pay off the extra bill a little at a time.

I entered the accounting office. Before I could speak, the bookkeeper looked up and smiled at me.

"Ah! Good morning, Mr. Hensley," she said brightly. "I think I know why *you're* here."

"You do?" I said, caught off-guard.

"You're here for your receipt, aren't you?" she continued. She located a piece of paper on her desk and handed it to me. "Here you are, sir. The bill for the blood transfusions for your wife is paid in full. Thank you!"

"P-paid . . . ?" I stammered. "But . . . but how?"

The bookkeeper looked surprised. "Didn't you know about it? Your friends from the university took care of the bill."

"That's not possible," I said in disbelief. "They don't have any money."

The bookkeeper chuckled.

"Oh, they didn't pay with money," she explained. "They used *barter.* Your wife needed six pints of blood, so six of your friends went to the Red Cross and donated that amount to replace what she had used. We credited their blood to your account, and that paid off your bill."

I stood there, amazed at such a marvelous answer to prayer, as well as at the loyalty and kindness of my friends.

I went to the university and there were my friends, all with small Band-Aids on the inner elbow of their left arms.

"I don't know what to say," I confessed. "You're all so wonderful."

"We didn't have any money," explained Dave, "so we paid the price in blood. They said it was worth more to them than money anyway. Money is something they can always raise, but it's only the blood that actually saves lives."

* * *

I have shared this story with many people during the past twenty-five years, for I believe God gave me that experience to dramatize a key aspect of our salvation experience. The Bible teaches us that "without shedding of blood there is no forgiveness" (Heb. 9:22 NASB), but through Christ "we have redemption through His blood, the forgiveness of our trespasses, according to the riches of His grace, which He lavished on us" (Eph. 1:7–8 NASB).

My six friends each gave a pint of blood so that, collectively, they could help save one person's life. That was a gracious and unselfish act of charity and kindness. But how much greater was the total sacrifice of Christ, giving His blood—His very life—to save the souls of all people.

I would have been a fool to reject the gift of the six pints of blood offered by my friends. Eagerly and willingly I accepted it.

But so, too, is it equally shortsighted and pathetically naive for millions of lost souls today to reject the gift of shed blood offered by Christ.

As my friend Dave noted, things like fame, money, prestige, and good deeds don't count in the end, for "it's only the *blood* that actually saves lives." We need to accept that gift.

SCRIPTURE VERSES TO PONDER

This righteousness from God comes through faith in Jesus Christ to all who believe. There is no difference, for all have sinned and fall short of the glory of God, and are justified freely by his grace through the redemption that came by Christ Jesus. God presented him as a sacrifice of atonement, through faith in his blood.

—Romans 3:22–25

In him we have redemption through his blood, the forgiveness of sins, in accordance with the riches of God's grace that he lavished on us with all wisdom and understanding.

—Ephesians 1:7–8

For God was pleased to have all his fullness dwell in him, and through him to reconcile to himself all things, whether things on earth or things in heaven, by making peace through his blood, shed on the cross.

—Colossians 1:19–20

To him who loves us and has freed us from our sins by his blood, and has made us to be a kingdom and priests to serve his God and Father—to him be glory and power for ever and ever!

—Revelation 1:5–6

QUESTIONS TO CONSIDER

1. Man's blood in recent years has become globally tainted with such infections as AIDS and hepatitis. Our blood has the life-giving power to sustain us, yet in man's sinful actions he often pollutes this power. What universal lessons about the "infection" of sin can we draw from this?

2. Various church denominations celebrate the Lord's supper at different times and in somewhat varied procedures; yet, this observance is known universally as "communion." What concepts of communion are obvious in the practice of God's children gathering to remind themselves of Christ's blood sacrifice?

3. The Old Testament tells us that Solomon sacrificed tens of thousands of sheep and cattle on blood altars in order to show honor to God. Yet, in all this massive sacrificing, he could not atone for the sins of people yet to be born. In what ways was the blood sacrifice of Jesus greater than all the blood sacrifices that had been offered previously?

4. The International Red Cross has as its theme, "Only Blood Saves Lives." What sort of similar themes do you think Christians could propose as appropriate messages for how we feel about the blood sacrifice Christ has provided for us?

SUGGESTED ADDITIONAL READING

McGrath, Alister. *Spirituality in an Age of Change: Rediscovering the Spirit of the Reformers.* Grand Rapids: Zondervan, 1994.

Olsson, Karl. *Passion.* New York: Harper and Row, 1963.

Piper, John. *Future Grace.* Sisters, Ore.: Questar, 1995.

Ryle, J. C. *Holiness: Its Nature, Hindrances, Difficulties and Roots.* 1883. Reprint, Grand Rapids: Baker, 1979.

CHAPTER 3

THE CINDERELLA
SYNDROME

One of the most familiar fairy tales is the story of Cinderella, the poor maiden who lost one of her glass slippers at the prince's ball. Cinderella's feet were so dainty and slender and beautiful, only she could fit into the glass slippers. As such, the prince used the slipper left behind as a way of locating his lost love.

As the prince searched for Cinderella, he recalled how her beautiful feet had danced more gracefully than any other lady's at the ball. He wanted to continue to enjoy this grace and beauty the rest of his life.

Upon finding the lowly Cinderella, the prince discovered that she was being held prisoner at a house where she was forced to do chores for a family that did not love her. The prince took Cinderella to the palace and married her. He freed her from her bonds and took her out of her prison. The prince knew that Cinderella's beautiful feet could only be beautiful *when they weren't locked behind closed doors.*

There's a lesson in that for us Christians, too.

You and I have feet just as beautiful as Cinderella's. True, our feet may not be able to wear glass slippers or even perform a waltz, but according to the Bible, that makes no difference. In Romans 10:15 we read, "How beautiful are the feet of them that preach the gospel of peace, and bring glad tidings of good things" (KJV).

Any time we walk up to a neighbor or friend or stranger and share what Christ has done in our lives, we have beautiful feet. Our feet are carrying the good news to the lost people of this world; our feet are conveying glad tidings. Indeed, this *is* something beautiful.

But if we never take that walk, our feet cannot become beautiful. Like Cinderella, our feet only become beautiful when they aren't locked behind closed doors.

During the 1960s a popular recording artist named Joe South had a hit single called "Walk a Mile." The song's chorus made this admonishment: "Before you accuse, criticize or abuse, walk a mile in my shoes."

Don't you appreciate the beautiful feet of people who have walked a mile in your shoes? I know *I* do. I once suffered a terrible facial disfigurement due to a damaged nerve. Several people expressed sympathy for my problem; one man, however, who had gone through an identical problem, drove fifty miles to see me and to tell me what to expect and how to cope with it. He truly had beautiful feet. I was extremely *glad* to have him there with me.

Jesus frequently used feet as a way of illustrating a lesson He was trying to teach. When He wanted to demonstrate humility, He got down on His knees and washed the feet of His disciples (John 13:5). When He wanted to teach forgiveness, He accepted the sinner woman's anointing of perfume on His feet and then He pardoned her of her sins (Luke 7:44–48). When He wanted to teach a lesson in evangelism, He said His feet had to walk through Samaria, even though this was forbidden by Jewish tradition (John 4:4).

Jesus was not guilty of being trapped in the "Cinderella Syndrome." He did not keep His feet behind closed doors. He used them to bring the Good News to lost souls. And He made the experience something beautiful for everyone He encountered.

What about you? Have you ever dreamed of winning a beauty pageant? If so, this is your big chance. All you have to do to win first prize in the Most Beautiful Feet Contest is to "step out" on behalf of Christ.

And that's no fairy tale.

SCRIPTURE VERSES TO PONDER

Make level paths for your feet
  and take only ways that are firm.
Do not swerve to the right or the left;
  keep your foot from evil.

—Proverbs 4:26–27

Then he turned toward the woman and said to Simon, "Do you see this woman? I came into your house. You did not give me any water for my feet, but she wet my feet with her tears and wiped them with her hair. You did not give me a kiss, but this woman, from the time I entered, has not stopped kissing my feet. You did not put oil on my head, but she has poured perfume on my feet. Therefore, I tell you, her many sins have been forgiven—for she loved much. But he who has forgiven little, loves little." Then Jesus said to her, "Your sins are forgiven."

—Luke 7:44–48

He came to Simon Peter, who said to him, "Lord, are you going to wash my feet?" Jesus replied, "You do not realize now what I am doing, but later you will understand." "No," said Peter, "you shall never wash my feet." Jesus answered, "Unless I wash you, you have no part with me."

—John 13:6–8

QUESTIONS TO CONSIDER

1. David proclaimed that even when he walked through the valley of the shadow of death, he would fear no evil, for he knew that the Lord walked with him. In what ways do you feel that the Lord is walking with you on a daily basis? How do you, conversely, sometimes stray from the straight and narrow way?

2. Robert Frost wrote a poem about a road divided. The poem stresses that the path one chooses will make all the difference in one's life. In what way is the theme of this poem similar to the choice each of us must make about following Christ or walking with Satan?

3. In the children's novel *Alice in Wonderland*, Alice comes to a fork in the road she has been following. She asks Humpty Dumpty, "Which way should I go?" He responds, "Where do you want to wind up?" She admits, "I don't know." To that, he says, "Oh, well then, any road will take you there." Is this similar to the way many people are when they refuse to accept Christ as their Savior? Don't they think one religion is the same as the next? How can we prove to such people how fundamentally wrong they are?

4. Jesus could have come to earth as a great king. Instead, He chose to walk among the sick, the poor, the uneducated, and the rejected people. What did His "walk" demonstrate about His "mission"?

SUGGESTED ADDITIONAL READING

Chambers, Oswald. *My Utmost for His Highest.* New York: Dodd, Mead, 1963.

Cowan, Charles E. *Streams in the Desert.* Grand Rapids: Zondervan, 1965.

Crawshaw, Dale. *Unleashing the Power of Joy: How to Recognize It, Grasp It, Claim It, Use It!* Chicago: Moody, 2002.

Goodrich, Donna, et al. *100 Plus Motivational Moments.* San Juan Capistrano, Calif.: Joy Publishing, 1991.

Mitchell, Curtis. *Let's Live! Christ in Everyday Life.* Old Tappan, N.J.: Revell, 1975.

Poland, Larry. *Rise to Conquer.* Chappaqua, N.Y.: Christian Herald Books, 1979.

CHAPTER 4

Don't Equate Complacency with Piety

Recently, after I gave a one-hour motivational speech at a gathering of Sunday school teachers and other church workers, I was approached by a lady who said coldly, "You need to learn that God is not keeping score regarding our accomplishments here on Earth. My heart is pure and my eyes are on Christ. That's what really matters, sir!"

I smiled, nodded my agreement, and said, "Indeed—for *your* life. But what about your next door neighbor and your dentist and your beautician? Are *their* hearts pure and are *their* eyes on Christ? If not, I guarantee you that your salvation is not going to save them. It is your witnessing that is going to make a difference. Don't equate confidence about your own spiritual situation with behavior that is glorifying to God. You are only halfway successful: you've found salvation for yourself, but now you must find it for others. Do some work!"

Noted management specialist Philip B. Crosby once stated, "Not failing is not the same as succeeding." At first reading, that statement may seem paradoxical. It holds a great truth, however. Phrased another way it might be said, "There is no status quo. You are either walking ahead or you are losing ground."

The same thing is true of the Christian life. There is no such thing as success in general, there is only success at *something*. Whatever your particular talent is, it should be directed toward some sort of ministry or service. If you are moving closer to achieving this goal, you are successful. If you are *not* walking toward the goal (or far worse, if you are drifting from it), you are failing.

Now note, I did not say your goal has to be something that turns the world upside down. All I said was that you should *have* a goal and you should be moving toward achieving it. God will be pleased with even the smallest efforts if they are made with the sincerest of sacrifice or devotion. A widow once gave her last bit of meal and oil to a prophet. A different widow donated two mites to the temple treasury. Both efforts were considered monumental deeds in God's eyes, though by man's standards they were insignificant contributions.

God does not want the service of a "blowhard." I once knew a man who boasted that after he received his holiday bonus, he was going to buy all new choir robes for the church. He also promised that if he was ever transferred to working second shift, he would help the pastor make calls on the needy. He talked of great things, but he never got around to doing any of them. Meanwhile, an elderly lady in our church worked faithfully as a nursery helper every Wednesday night and every Sunday morning. Her small work efforts were of far greater value than the unachieved big plans of the talkative man.

Ecclesiastes 5:3–4 explains, "For a dream [goal] cometh through the multitude of business [work]; and a fool's voice is known by [a] multitude of words. When thou vowest a vow unto God, defer not to pay it; for he hath no pleasure in fools" (KJV).

God is pleased with successful workers. When David raised up a great army (his work) and went out to reclaim the land of Israel, God gave him victory. When Solomon built the temple (his work), God blessed it. When Joshua attacked the inhabitants of Canaan (his work), God gave him the land. When Nehemiah developed a plan to rebuild the wall of Jerusalem (his work), God protected the workers and provided the materials.

Conversely, God "hath no pleasure in fools" who neglect to do the work He has called them to do. When Moses was too meek to speak before Pharaoh, God took the gift of oratory away and gave it to Aaron. When Jonah ran from the assignment to preach in Nineveh, God created a great fish to swallow him and then vomit him on a seashore. When John Mark could not maintain the pace of aggressive evangelism that Paul was setting, Paul dismissed him from the work.

God's people and His churches are not honoring Him when they are complacent and neutral. God gave a message to the church at Laodicea that needs to be heeded by all churches and all Christians: "I know thy works, that thou art neither cold nor hot: I would thou wert cold or hot. So then because thou art lukewarm, and neither cold nor hot, I will spue thee out of my mouth" (Rev. 3:15–16 KJV). It is amazing how similar this sounds to Crosby's admonition that not failing is not the same as succeeding. God's will is for us *to succeed* at a God-honoring work.

Jesus succeeded in all He set out to accomplish here on Earth. Not only that, but He spent time teaching His followers that they, too, should succeed at some work for God the Father. It is not enough to warm a pew on Sunday mornings. There is work to do.

Jesus explained it once with a little story (Luke 13:6–9). A man owned a lovely orchard which gave him many delicious fruits to eat and sell. Amidst the orchard, however, was one large tree that had many branches, many lush green leaves, and many deep and strong roots; yet, this tree never produced any fruit. The landowner had been patient with the tree for three growing seasons, but in none of those years did it yield figs.

Finally, the landowner told his head gardener to chop down the tree, clear out the roots, and plant a new tree on that spot so that eventually there would be fruit coming from that section of the orchard. The head gardener understood his employer's frustration, but he suggested an alternative plan.

He asked that he be allowed to irrigate the land around the tree so that more water could get to the roots and that he be allowed to fertilize the soil so that nutrients could get into the tree. He promised his employer that if this did not succeed in helping the tree bear fruit, then, indeed, the tree should be chopped down.

We should take this as a warning. If we are a large but unproductive tree planted in one of God's vineyards (a church, a Christian youth group, an evangelistic outreach), we are not in a neutral position; we are actually taking up room where someone more productive could be helping and ministering.

God the Father, as landowner, may choose to remove us and eliminate the hindrance we are causing. Christ, as the patient gardener, wants to give us yet another chance. He wants to encourage us to sink our roots into God's Word and become productive for His ministry. However, if we will not heed His suggestions and encouragements, then He will agree that it may be best for us to be removed from our orchard of ministry.

How about you? Are you succeeding at anything? Sooner or later, harvest time will come. When it does, what will you show: abundance or barrenness? It has to be one or the other, because not failing is not the same as succeeding.

SCRIPTURE VERSES TO PONDER

. . . be ready to do the work of the LORD.

—Numbers 8:11

Moreover, when God gives any man wealth and possessions, and enables him to enjoy them, to accept his lot and be happy in his work—this is a gift of God. He seldom reflects on the days of his life, because God keeps him occupied with gladness of heart.

—Ecclesiastes 5:19–20

A curse on him who is lax in doing the LORD's work!

—Jeremiah 48:10

As long as it is day, we must do the work of him who sent me. Night is coming, when no one can work.

—John 9:4

If any man builds on this foundation using gold, silver, costly stones, wood, hay or straw, his work will be shown for what it is, because the Day will bring it to light. It will be revealed with fire, and the fire will test the quality of each man's work. If what he has built survives, he will receive his reward. If it is burned up, he will suffer loss.

—1 Corinthians 3:12–15

QUESTIONS TO CONSIDER

1. Can you recall a time when you were struggling to serve the Lord in a particular ministry and it did not seem to be going well? Was it hard to continue to work for the Lord when you saw so little progress and so few positive results? How did you feel about this? Did you wonder if you had failed the Lord . . . or if He had failed you? What conclusions did you finally come to?

2. What do you think Dwight L. Moody meant when he once stated that he became weary in the service of the Lord, but he never became weary *of* the service of the Lord?

3. What is the most difficult aspect of serving the Lord for you, personally—witnessing? Maintaining a living testimony? Teaching a class at church? Serving in a church leadership position? Maintaining daily devotional time and a consistent prayer life? Knowing that each of these is something proper to do, why can they, nevertheless, seem to be wearisome at times? What can we do about that?

4. When you are serving the Lord in a ministry that is a joy to you, why does it feel as though you aren't even working? What ministries are you currently involved in where this is true of you? How did you discover these ways of serving the Lord? What does having such joyous feelings about your service in these areas teach you about how, when, and where you should serve God?

SUGGESTED ADDITIONAL READING

Bright, John. *The Kingdom of God.* Nashville: Abingdon, 1953.

Hale, J. Russell. *The Unchurched: Who They Are and Why They Stay That Way.* San Francisco: Harper and Row, 1980.

Ingram, Chip. *Holy Ambition: What It Takes to Make a Difference for God.* Chicago: Moody, 2002.

Walrath, Douglas. *Leading Churches Through Change.* Nashville: Abingdon, 1979.

Worley, Robert C. *A Gathering of Strangers: Understanding the Life of Your Church.* Philadelphia: Westminster, 1976.

Yeakley, Flavil R. *Why Churches Grow.* Nashville: Anderson Press, 1977.

CHAPTER 5

DAD WAS BETTER THAN
A TEXTBOOK

Remember how, when you were a kid, you thought your dad was the smartest person in the world . . . he knew the answers to everything? Well, in my case, it turned out to be true.

And that's really quite remarkable when you consider that my father had to drop out of school in the eighth grade, that he enlisted in the Navy at age seventeen and later finished his high school equivalency course while also working full-time.

Now *me* . . . well, I have four university degrees hanging on my wall, including a Ph.D. with "distinguished honors." I've had the opportunity to study under the finest scholars at the finest schools money can provide.

Yet, here's the truth of the matter: I've never listened to a single lecture nor read any particular book that has taught me any more about what life's *truly valuable* lessons are than the things I learned by just watching my dad.

For example: I'm well past my thirty-third wedding anniversary year, and my wife and I are as much in love today as we were when we first said, "I do." I've cared for my wife and encouraged her and done everything I could do to make her feel like a queen all these years. Similarly, she has been my partner and cheerleader through thick and thin. Life has handed us some challenges, but we've always pulled together to get through any and all trials.

But did I learn how to be a good husband from a textbook? No way. I just watched my dad and copied him. He always held my mother, kissed her, told her how nice she looked, bragged about her cooking, took her with him on business trips, shared jokes with her, asked her advice on personal and career matters, and remained faithful to her all these years. They had their spats and disagreements, as all couples do, but my father never struck my mother, never yelled at her. You could just tell by the way he treated her that she was special to him. And that same behavior has worked wonders in my own marriage.

The same holds true for raising children. I have two kids, both grown now. My son graduated with an MBA from a leading university; while in school he also did a full hitch in the United States Marine Corps Reserves, including war-zone duty in Kuwait during "Operation Iraqi Freedom"; he bought his own car; and he even found time to do some Sunday school teaching. My daughter was never off the honor roll since first grade; she earned stacks of awards and honors both as a writer and as a musician; she participated in drama and choir in college; she traveled to Australia, England, Russia, and Ireland; and she now has a great career as an elementary school music teacher.

OK, so who gets the credit for this? Perhaps it should go to the college courses I took in philosophy of education and in child psychology? Not a chance. Again, it was just me copying my dad. He never did anything with me or my brother or my sister because he'd learned about it in a "psych" class; he did everything with us because he was crazy about us.

If we had ball games, he was in the stands cheering. If it was PTA night, he went along with my mom. If my sister had a recital, he was in the front row.

He taught me how to play the guitar, prepare a Sunday school lesson, and drive a car. He hired me to work for his company during the summers I was off from college. He wrote to me every day when I was serving for a year in Vietnam. He loaned me the money for a down payment on my first home. And to this day, even though I'm in my fifties, my dad still hugs and kisses me whenever we get together. He has always made me feel like the most marvelous person he has ever known—and it has made me do everything in my power to be worthy of that.

What was my dad's secret for raising good kids? Simply this: Log a lot of time with them and make them feel special. It's a system that works. I know. I've used it.

One final thing: During the past thirty-five years I've been active in church as a youth leader, Sunday school teacher, deacon, elder, church treasurer, and missions liaison. At first consideration, I thought that this, too, might be me just following the patterns of my dad. After all, he was always the fellow who headed the church's annual fund-raiser for the orphans at Christmas, or who made sure the pastor had his glasses adjusted correctly (my dad was an optician by trade).

But upon further consideration, I don't think that's the case. I'm now convinced that my service to God through the ministries of His church is given because of my desire to show my love and devotion to Him. I am absolutely convinced that my heavenly Father loves me, is concerned about me, and cares for me. In return, I want to do everything in my power to be worthy of that love and care. So, I serve Him.

What has convinced me, however, that my heavenly Father can have such a deep love for me is the fact that I've had an earthly father who has always loved me so genuinely. If a mere man, like my dad, can love that intensely, how much greater must be the love that my Creator has for me! It's mind-boggling just trying to consider it.

I have two wonderful fathers. The one on earth, by his actions and faith and love, has given me a glimpse of the One in heaven. I hope that *my* children will one day be able to say the same thing about me, for that would be the greatest legacy any man could ever desire.

SCRIPTURE VERSES TO PONDER

Each of you must respect his mother and father. . . . I am the
LORD your God.

—Leviticus 19:3

A wise son brings joy to his father.

—Proverbs 10:1

Listen to your father, who gave you life,
    and do not despise your mother when she is old.
Buy the truth and do not sell it;
    get wisdom, discipline and understanding.
The father of a righteous man has great joy;
    he who has a wise son delights in him.

—Proverbs 23:22–24

Endure hardship as discipline; God is treating you as sons.
For what son is not disciplined by his father? If you are not
disciplined (and everyone undergoes discipline), then you are
illegitimate children and not true sons. Moreover, we have all
had human fathers who disciplined us and we respected them
for it. How much more should we submit to the Father of our
spirits and live! Our fathers disciplined us for a little while as
they thought best; but God disciplines us for our good, that
we may share in his holiness.

—Hebrews 12:7–10

QUESTIONS TO CONSIDER

1. There were once two identical twin boys. Their father was a
    drunkard who did little to care for his wife and sons. He died of
    alcoholism when the boys were teenagers. Later in life, one boy
    became a huge success as a college graduate, a business leader, a

fine family man, and a pillar of his community. The other twin became an alcoholic, drifting aimlessly, never accomplishing anything and slowly ruining his health. Both twins were interviewed by a social worker and asked, "Why do you think you turned out the way you did in life?" Each boy, speaking separately, responded, "With a father like mine, what else could I have expected to be?" Note: What lessons can we draw from this little story?

2. Have you reared a family? What have you noticed about the way your children mimic your actions, copy your words, even want to dress up in your clothes? What does this imply about how our actions speak louder than words as parents?

3. Recent sociological studies have found that children who stay in a home, even where the parents are dysfunctional, have a better overall sense of "belonging." What does this surprising fact seem to indicate about God's plan that the traditional family (father, mother, children) should stay together as a unit? How has society in recent years tried to undermine this concept? What can we do to preserve God's intent for the family structure?

SUGGESTED ADDITIONAL READING

Field, David. *Marriage Personalities.* Eugene, Ore.: Harvest House, 1986.

McCrary, James Leslie. *Freedom and Growth in Marriage.* New York: John Wiley and Sons, 1980.

Snyder, Chuck and Barb. *Incompatibility: Grounds for a Great Marriage.* Phoenix: Questar, 1988.

Werner, Hazen G. *The Bible and the Family.* Nashville: Abingdon, 1966.

York, Frank, and Jan LaRue. *Protecting Your Child in an X-Rated World.* Wheaton, Ill.: Tyndale House, 2002.

CHAPTER 6

THE YOUTHFUL LEADER

He was twenty-five years old when he became king.
—2 Kings 18:2

Even though at age twenty Abe Lincoln was the youngest man among his platoon of recruits enlisted to fight in the Blackfoot Indian Wars, the general had promoted Lincoln to the rank of platoon captain. At first this totally baffled everyone in the regiment. Why, they wondered, would the general select this young farm boy as a leader when there were so many other men—pioneers, scouts, military veterans, frontiersmen—who seemed to have much better qualifications?

"Lincoln shall be your leader," explained the general, "because he is the only man among you who can read and write. When I send my orders to this platoon, I want to be sure that they will be totally understood, correctly explained, and properly obeyed. Forget about the fact that Lincoln is young. Remember only that he speaks my words and, therefore, must be obeyed."

Young Abe rose to the challenge. He drilled his men, gave them their rations and ammunition, answered their questions, and even wrote letters back home to their relatives for them. Abe also read orders to the men from the general and saw to it that his platoon was always where it was supposed to be, when it was supposed to be, and outfitted the way it was supposed to be. Soon, the old veterans over-looked the fact that Lincoln was young. They grew to appreciate his diligence and dedication. They obeyed him faithfully without ever having to be reminded of the general's order.

In following our Great Captain, Jesus Christ, and obeying His directives, we, too, can be of greatest service to God and to our fellow man. Obedience evolves into wisdom.

SCRIPTURE VERSES TO PONDER

> So then, banish anxiety from your heart
>   and cast off the troubles of your body,
>   for youth and vigor are meaningless.
> Remember your Creator
>   in the days of your youth,
>   before the days of trouble come
>   and the years approach when you will say,
> "I find no pleasure in them."
>   —Ecclesiastes 11:10–12:1

Similarly, encourage the young men to be self-controlled. In everything set them an example by doing what is good. In your teaching show integrity, seriousness and soundness of speech that cannot be condemned, so that those who oppose you may be ashamed because they have nothing bad to say about us.
                                        —Titus 2:6–8

Young men, in the same way be submissive to those who are older. All of you, clothe yourselves with humility toward one another, because,

> "God opposes the proud
>   but gives grace to the humble."

Humble yourselves, therefore, under God's mighty hand, that
he may lift you up in due time.

—1 Peter 5:5–6

QUESTIONS TO CONSIDER

1. "Children should be seen and not heard" is an adage that has
   been around for many decades. In what ways does this agree
   with or go against what the Bible has to say about properly training our young people?
2. In selecting people for church leadership roles, how do you feel
   the question of one's age should be considered: By actual years
   of age? By years of salvation experience? By previous years of
   service to the church? By a combination of all of these?
3. In biblical times, some kings were crowned and anointed at ages
   as young as twelve, fifteen, or twenty-one years old. Which young
   kings can you recall from the Old Testament? How were their
   lives of service to God, or of disgrace to themselves and their
   heritage? (Consider Josiah, Solomon, and others.)
4. In many ways modern society is trying to make young people
   grow up too quickly. What examples of this do you see in advertising, television programs, motion pictures, and even in the
   way young people are educated today? How should we, as older
   Christians, deal with these circumstances?
5. As church leaders, teachers, pastors, elders, and deacons, how
   can we be walking examples of Christian maturity?

SUGGESTED ADDITIONAL READING

Dobson, James C. *Straight Talk to Men and Their Wives.* Waco, Tex.:
     Word, 1980.
Foster, Richard J. *Celebration of Discipline.* San Francisco: Harper and
     Row, 1978.

Kay, Ellie. *Money Doesn't Grow on Trees: Teaching Your Kids the Value of a Buck.* Minneapolis: Bethany House, 2002.

McDowell, Josh, and Bob Hostetler. *Right from Wrong.* Dallas: Word, 1994.

Schuller, Robert Anthony. *Getting Through the Going-Through Stage.* Nashville: Nelson, 1986.

Thurman, Chris. *The Truths We Must Believe.* Nashville: Nelson, 1991.

CHAPTER 7

A MATTER OF INTERNAL
SECURITY

On what are you basing this confidence of yours?
—2 Kings 18:19

Tom Yoder was frustrated. For six months as a Peace Corps volunteer he had worked diligently to earn the trust of a tribe of native Africans. He had many new skills that he eagerly wanted to share with them. He had tools for them, new concepts about farming, plans for irrigation ditches, lessons about crop rotation, and even a new shipping schedule for the selling and delivery of their surplus fruits and vegetables. However, the locals did not trust this outsider.

One day a young child came to Yoder's hut. The boy pointed to the far end of the village and said, "The family that lives in that hut has fallen ill. The people of this village have abandoned them to die. But the children are my friends. Can you help them?"

Yoder rushed to the forbidden hut, entered, and immediately realized that the family had contracted yellow fever. He returned to his hut and retrieved blankets, fresh food, hot water bottles, medicine, and clean clothes. For the next six days Yoder bathed, fed, and nursed the family until each was strong enough to be transported ninety miles to a hospital. All the family members returned later, completely healed.

The villagers then called Yoder the "Great Fearless One." From then on they listened to him and accepted all of his ideas on farming.

Weeks later, when Yoder sat down to record this amazing turn of events in his journal, he wrote, "It is easy to be fearless when you have been vaccinated against a disease."

Fear and insecurity are part of today's life; but Christ died that we might conquer fear. Followers of Christ have substituted all fear of death with God's promise of everlasting security. Christians do not fear the valley.

SCRIPTURE VERSES TO PONDER

David said to the Philistine, "You come against me with sword and spear and javelin, but I come against you in the name of the LORD Almighty, the God of the armies of Israel, whom you have defied. This day the LORD will hand you over to me, and I'll strike you down and cut off your head. Today I will give the carcasses of the Philistine army to the birds of the air and the beasts of the earth, and the whole world will know that there is a God in Israel. All those gathered here will know that it is not by sword or spear that the LORD saves; for the battle is the LORD's, and he will give all of you into our hands."

—1 Samuel 17:45–47

Shadrach, Meshach and Abednego replied to the king, "O Nebuchadnezzar, we do not need to defend ourselves before you in this matter. If we are thrown into the blazing furnace, the God we serve is able to save us from it, and he will rescue us from your hand, O king. But even if he does not, we want you to know, O king, that we will not serve your gods or worship the image of gold you have set up."

—Daniel 3:16–18

QUESTIONS TO CONSIDER

1. Consider the stories of bravery as evidenced by Moses, Daniel, Shadrach, Meshach, Abednego, David, Gideon, Peter, Paul, and other great heroes of the Bible. What enabled them to be so strong both emotionally and spiritually? What elements of their character should we emulate today? What can we do to develop the same sort of faith and confidence they had?

2. There also are stories of Bible cowards. Why was Jonah too afraid to do as God told him to regarding the city of Nineveh? Why did Moses suddenly become too afraid to speak in front of Pharaoh? Why did John Mark desert Paul during the first missionary journey? Why did Thomas lack faith to believe that Jesus had risen from the dead? What elements of the lives of these people are similar to our own lives? What can we do to avoid behaving in a cowardly fashion?

3. Often people are drawn to us because they admire the way we live. They respect us for our strength of character, our personal disciplines, and our moral behavior. This allows us to share the gospel with them. How important, then, is it for us to be a "walking testimony" of our faith in Christ? In what specific ways can we exemplify this faith at home, on the job, and in our communities?

SUGGESTED ADDITIONAL READING

Colson, Charles. *The Body.* Dallas, Tex.: Word, 1992.

McDowell, Josh. *More Than a Carpenter.* Wheaton: Tyndale House, 1978.

Ten Boom, Corrie. *The Hiding Place.* Old Tappan, N.J.: Revell, 1971.

Thurman, Chris. *The Lies We Believe.* Nashville: Nelson, 1989.

Van Kempen, Case. *Hard Questions People Ask About the Christian Faith.* Colorado Springs: Faith Alive, 2002.

Woodridge, John D., ed. *Renewing Your Mind in a Secular World.* Chicago: Moody, 1985.

CHAPTER 8

The Eloquence of the Silent Orator

But the people held their peace, and answered him not a word.
—2 Kings 18:36 KJV

What we *are* often speaks far louder that what we *say*.

Back at the turn of the twentieth century, an elderly Kentucky farmer rode to church each Sunday morning in his buckboard. On purpose, he went the long way so as to come into town from the far end. There he would stop each time at the livery stable and ask his long-time friend, the blacksmith, to attend church with him.

This only amused the rugged blacksmith who would laugh, shake his head, and respond emphatically, "No! And quit coming by here every Sunday morning. I've got work to do, and you know my answer never changes!"

The farmer continued to stop every Sunday, however. He tried every form of persuasion he could think of: he begged, warned, implored, teased, threatened, and encouraged. His words all failed. The blacksmith continued to ignore the farmer's warnings and pleadings.

Finally, one Sunday, with tear-filled eyes, the farmer approached the livery stable. His heart was burdened for the blacksmith's soul, but he could think of no new way to approach the man.

Slowly, he dismounted the seat of the buckboard, trying to form some words. The sorrow over his failure to reach this man for Christ was overwhelming. He walked to the blacksmith, tears rolling down his cheeks and a lump in his throat. He could not speak. His grief was too genuine, too severe.

The old farmer just squeezed the blacksmith's hands and walked away from him, still sobbing.

In an instant the blacksmith removed his work bib and ran after the man. "Wait! I'll go with you," he called out. "Your silence is more convincing than your words ever were."

Our God has an unlimited storehouse of plans; some are quietly powerful. "Be silent, O all flesh, before the LORD" (Zech. 2:13 KJV).

SCRIPTURE VERSES TO PONDER

I said, "I will watch my ways
   and keep my tongue from sin;
I will put a muzzle on my mouth
   as long as the wicked are in my presence."

—Psalm 39:1

Even a fool is thought wise if he keeps silent,
   and discerning if he holds his tongue.

—Proverbs 17:28

There is a time for everything,
   and a season for every activity under heaven: . . .
   a time to be silent and a time to speak.

—Ecclesiastes 3:1, 7

But just as you excel in everything—in faith, in speech, in knowledge, in complete earnestness and in your love for us— see that you also excel in this grace of giving.

—2 Corinthians 8:7

Don't let anyone look down on you because you are young, but set an example for the believers in speech, in life, in love, in faith and in purity.

—1 Timothy 4:12

QUESTIONS TO CONSIDER

1. Have you ever found that you can comfort someone who is grieving over a lost loved one just by being present? What is it about the touch of a hand, a smile, or an encouraging hug that is equal to any words you might say?
2. Do you worry at times that what you say when you are witnessing has become a "boiler plate" presentation? What can we do to ensure that the words we share about Christ will be the precise words needed by each individual we talk to and not just a rehearsed presentation?
3. There is an old saying: "Silence is golden." In what particular ways might this be true of Christian behavior, specifically in regard to such things as criticism, advising, evaluating, judging, and encouraging?
4. We are often told that what we do speaks louder than what we say. Can you think of instances, both good and bad, in which something you or someone else did wound up making a major impression on another person?
5. When Jesus washed the feet of his disciples, how did this action speak louder than words? In Christ's parable, when the Good Samaritan cared for the injured stranger, how did his actions speak louder than words?

SUGGESTED ADDITIONAL READING

Arnold, Henri. *Freedom from Sinful Thoughts: Christ Alone Breaks the Curse.* Rifton, N.Y.: Plough Publishing, 1973.

Dreisbach, Bruce. *The Jesus Plan*. Colorado Springs: WaterBrook, 2002.

Kelsey, Morton T. *The Other Side of Silence: A Guide to Christian Meditation*. New York: Paulist, 1976.

Merton, Thomas. *Contemplative Prayer*. Garden City, N.Y.: Doubleday, 1972.

O'Connor, Elizabeth. *Search for Silence*. Waco, Tex.: Word, 1971.

Rohrbach, Peter-Thomas. *Conversation with Christ*. Chicago: Fides Publishers, 1956.

CHAPTER 9

PROPER NAVIGATION

The way of the wicked he turneth upside down.
—Psalm 146:9 KJV

Jon Skillman was a television reporter who had a reputation for getting the inside view of whatever story he was reporting on. Thus, it was with great excitement that he accepted an offer from the U.S. Air Force to ride in the back seat of a jet fighter. Here was a way to get a bird's-eye view of aerial acrobatics and combat procedures.

Skillman was himself a pilot of small fixed-wing aircraft, and he was proud of his knowledge of flying. To fly in a jet was a dream come true for him, both as a journalist and as an aviator.

Skillman sat in the back seat of the two-seated cockpit and strapped himself in. He had been briefed on the mock attack run he and the pilot would be going on.

"Ready, Mr. Skillman?" asked the pilot.

"Let 'er rip, Captain," Jon responded excitedly.

The jet roared into the sky, did four rollovers, a power dive, and then climbed into a cloud bank.

"Wow! That was really some fantastic maneuvering!" Skillman said by radio to the pilot. "I almost lost my stomach. Hey, for a minute there I didn't even know which end was up."

"You still don't," responded the pilot.

At that moment the jet cleared the cloud bank and rolled into an upright position. Skillman saw that they had been flying upside down for several minutes. Only the pilot, by reading his instruments, really had known up from down.

God's Word serves as a compass to guide us. The world's answers to problems often send us head-over-heels into a topsy-turvy gyration of confusion. In following Christ, however, we stay on the right course. Jesus said, "I am the way."

SCRIPTURE VERSES TO PONDER

I run in the path of your commands,
    for you have set my heart free.
Teach me, O LORD, to follow your decrees.
                                        — Psalm 119:32–33

The way of the sluggard is blocked with thorns,
    but the path of the upright is a highway.
                                        —Proverbs 15:19

A man's steps are directed by the LORD.
    How then can anyone understand his own way?
                                        —Proverbs 20:24

Come, let us go up to the mountain of the LORD,
    to the house of the God of Jacob.
He will teach us his ways,
    so that we may walk in his paths.
                                        —Isaiah 2:3

To this you were called, because Christ suffered for you, leaving you an example, that you should follow in his steps.
                                        —1 Peter 2:21

QUESTIONS TO CONSIDER

1. Have you charted your life for Christ? Are you on the right path in your service to Him? What sort of navigational checks can you make to be sure you truly are on "the straight and narrow path"?
2. Can you recall some individuals from the Bible who began their lives totally walking with God, yet later strayed from that path? How did this affect both their early and later years? (Be sure to consider David, Solomon, and Peter.)
3. One time Paul admonished Peter for his behavior when Peter was associating with Jews rather than Gentile converts. Do you have a friend who will "set you straight" if you start to change course in your following of the Lord?
4. Do you keep a journal or diary of daily events? If so, if you were to go back and read some entries from ten years ago, five years ago, or one year ago, would you find that your walk with God has been consistent or varied? Either way, what makes it so, do you think?
5. What sort of practices do you maintain to help you stay on the right path for God? Daily Bible reading? Church attendance? Devotions and prayer? Fellowship with like-minded believers?

SUGGESTED ADDITIONAL READING

Bonhoeffer, Dietrich. *The Way to Freedom.* New York: Harper and Row, 1966.

Bounds, E. M. *Power Through Prayer.* Chicago: Moody, 1939.

Kelly, Thomas R. *A Testament of Devotion.* New York: Harper and Brothers, 1941.

Laubach, Frank C. *Prayer, the Mightiest Force in the World.* New York: Revell, 1946.

Radcliffe, Lynn J. *Making Prayer Real.* New York: Abingdon-Cokesbury, 1952.

Stevens, R. Paul. *Seven Days of Faith: Every Day Alive with God.* Colorado Springs: NavPress, 2002.

CHAPTER 10

PEACEFUL COEXISTENCE

He grants peace to your borders.

—Psalm 147:14

The United States and Canada share the longest unguarded border in the world. From Maine to Washington State, the boundary is respected by both nations and is preserved with tranquillity. Never since British colonial days have these two nations engaged in war with each other. In fact, through treaties, each nation has promised to come to the rescue of the other should either come under attack by a foreign power.

What a contrast this is to the many decades the city of Berlin was divided by a cement wall, barbed wire, mine fields, searchlights, and guards with machine guns. Though every U.S. President from Truman to Ford had spoken against the wall and had tried to bring political pressure to secure its removal, it wasn't until 1989 that it finally was torn down. Only then was peaceful coexistence reestablished between East and West Berlin and, ultimately, a reuniting of the entire nation was gained.

Since then, other walls have fallen all over the world. The USSR has disbanded its regional alliances; South Africa has relinquished white rule; and some of the Irish militants have ceased their violent actions against Great Britain. Major changes in the geo-political world are more commonplace than ever before. The workings of God, who sets up and removes kings and governments, are evident everywhere.

The motto of the United States is, "In God We Trust." God has returned this honor by keeping warrior nations at a distance and drawing friendly nations to our borders. Historically, the nations that have praised the one true God have been rewarded with great abundance and prosperity. Of late, America has seen its borders penetrated by alien invaders, as with the attack on the Twin Trade Towers in New York City on September 11, 2001. Such events should drive us to our knees, seeking the continued blessing of God for our nation.

God brings peace both to nations and to families. His grace is able to break down barriers, heal old wounds, and unite former enemies. Tranquillity is a gift from God. Receiving it begins by turning to Him.

SCRIPTURE VERSES TO PONDER

If you follow my decrees and are careful to obey my commands, I will send you rain in its season, and the ground will yield its crops and the trees of the field their fruit. Your threshing will continue until grape harvest and the grape harvest will continue until planting, and you will eat all the food you want and live in safety in your land. I will grant peace in the land, and you will lie down and no one will make you afraid. I will remove savage beasts from the land, and the sword will not pass through your country.

—Leviticus 26:3–6

The LORD gives strength to his people;
    the LORD blesses his people with peace.

—Psalm 29:11

He will proclaim peace to the nations.
    His rule will extend from sea to sea
and from the River to the ends of the earth.

—Zechariah 9:10

God has called us to live in peace.

—1 Corinthians 7:15

QUESTIONS TO CONSIDER

1. Have you ever talked to a war veteran after he or she has returned from many months of battle? Why does it seem hard for such people to accept the fact that they are now safe at home and no longer in danger? How is this a parallel of new converts who, though saved and now true believers, often have some misgivings about their eternal salvation or about the unchanging love of Christ?

2. What has been the value of treaties throughout history? For the most part they have proved to be worthless. The treaties between the U.S. government and the frontier Indians were violated in many ways, nearly to the extinction of some entire tribes of Native Americans. The treaties Hitler made with England and with the Soviet Union were violated within weeks of their signings. What lessons can we draw from this about man's ability to find peace on his own terms? How does this underscore the need for finding peace with God first?

3. During the 1960s, thousands of college students in the United States, Europe, and Asia organized "peace movements" to protest wars. Ironically, their demonstrations often ended in clashes with the police, fights, arrests, and injuries. Although their hearts seemed to be in the right place, what mistakes were these young people making? How is peace, apart from a relationship with God, impossible?

SUGGESTED ADDITIONAL READING

Bonhoeffer, Dietrich. *The Cost of Discipleship.* New York: Macmillan, 1963.

Erwin, Gayle D. *The Jesus Style.* Waco, Tex.: Word, 1985.

Lewis, C. S. *Surprised by Joy.* New York: Inspiration Press, 1987.

Miller, Holly G., and Dennis E. Hensley. *How to Stop Living for the Applause: Help for Women Who Need to Be Perfect.* Ann Arbor: Servant Publications, 1990.

Thomas, Kim. *Living in the Sacred Now.* Eugene, Ore.: Harvest House, 2002.

Wallis, Arthur. *God's Chosen Fast.* Fort Washington, Pa.: Christian Literature Crusade, 1971.

CHAPTER 11

THE VALUE OF A GOOD NAME

Let every one that nameth the name of Christ
depart from iniquity.
—2 Timothy 2:19 KJV

Judah Ben-Hur is the prosperous Jewish hero of Lew Wallace's Bible-era novel *Ben-Hur*. Though wealthy and educated, Judah walks with his head lowered whenever he travels in areas of his city that are patrolled by the Roman conquerors who invaded his land. He does not speak unless spoken to, for only Roman citizens have rights and privileges in captive nations.

Through a series of odd circumstances, Judah is put into prison and then made a galley slave on a Roman warship. During a great sea battle, Judah saves the life of a very influential Roman military commander. As a reward, the man declares Judah to be his adopted son. He lets Judah wear a ring signifying his new social rank and power. Thereafter, everywhere Judah walks, he holds his head high. People bow respectfully before him. Roman soldiers obey his orders. Politicians try to gain his favor. As the heir of a Roman proconsul, Judah receives respect from everyone he encounters.

Christians, too, are the heirs of great nobility. Our heavenly Father is the King of Kings and Lord of Lords. He owns the cattle on a thousand hills (and the hills). He is the Ruler of the earth and of all who dwell on it.

More powerful, however, than a Roman proconsul's limited power is God's power to grant eternal life to all who seek Him. The heavenly kingdom awaits all who accept the kinship of Christ. We are joint heirs with Jesus.

SCRIPTURE VERSES TO PONDER

But I said to you, "You will possess their land; I will give it to you as an inheritance, a land flowing with milk and honey." I am the LORD your God, who has set you apart.

—Leviticus 20:24

LORD, you have assigned me my portion and my cup;
    you have made my lot secure.
The boundary lines have fallen for me in pleasant places;
    surely I have a delightful inheritance.

—Psalm 16:5–6

For of this you can be sure: No immoral, impure or greedy person—such a man is an idolater—has any inheritance in the kingdom of Christ and of God.

—Ephesians 5:5

And we pray this in order that you may live a life worthy of the Lord and may please him in every way: bearing fruit in every good work, growing in the knowledge of God, being strengthened with all power according to his glorious might so that you may have great endurance and patience, and joyfully giving thanks to the Father, who has qualified you to share in the inheritance of the saints in the kingdom of light.

—Colossians 1:10–12

QUESTIONS TO CONSIDER

1. Certain names—Vanderbilt, Hughes, Trump—have carried with them an immediate recognition factor. People related to these families are proud of their success and fame. How much more should we be pleased in knowing that we are God's children? How can we express our joy over this?

2. How should knowing that we are part of the family of God regulate our actions, thoughts, plans, and daily walk? In what ways do our actions speak louder than our words?

3. What we inherit tangibly (money, homes, cars, jewelry) from our parents or other relatives often is not of equal worth to what we inherit from them in the way of moral lessons and Christian values. Why is this so? Knowing this, how can we pass on to our children and grandchildren inheritances that are worth more than tangible goods?

4. In what ways is the Bible a special inheritance that we have had passed down to us by God and by previous generations of believers? How can we most "profit" from our use of this inheritance? How can we, in turn, pass it on to a new generation?

SUGGESTED ADDITIONAL READING

McMinn, Don. *Strategic Living.* Grand Rapids: Baker, 1983.

Morton, Kelsey. *Caring: How Can We Love One Another?* New York: Paulist, 1981.

Shaeffer, Edith. *What Is a Family?* Old Tappan: Revell, 1975.

Thurman, Chris, and David Ferguson. *The Pursuit of Intimacy.* Nashville: Nelson, 1993.

Wheat, Ed. *Love Life for Every Married Couple.* Grand Rapids: Zondervan, 1978.

Willmer, Wesley K., with Martyn Smith. *God and Your Stuff.* Colorado Springs: NavPress, 2002.

CHAPTER 12

WHEN HEAVEN DOWNSIZES

I had been trying to witness to my neighbor Wade about his need of Christ in his life. But because things were going well for Wade, he paid little attention to me.

"Hey, I go to church on Easter and at Christmas," Wade would say, chuckling. "My wife and daughter go even more often than that. No lightning bolts have fallen out of the sky on me. I'm doing OK."

I shook my head. "You're just 'playing church,'" I said. "You may be appeasing yourself, but you're not fooling God."

"Look," he said, "I work hard all week, lots of overtime, so I'm exhausted by the time Sunday rolls around. God isn't going to begrudge me a little shut-eye."

"I'm not talking about church attendance," I responded. "You have no day-to-day relationship with Christ. All you care about is putting in extra hours so that you can buy a motorcycle and a fishing boat and a large screen TV. None of that will redeem your soul."

Wade yawned. "Me and God, we're cool," he said. "I ain't robbing no banks or killing anybody. God knows I'm pretty decent. When my number comes up, my record will get me through those pearly gates.

It's like merit pay at the factory—the harder you work, the more valuable you are to the boss."

"You can't earn your way into heaven," I argued. "Only by accepting Christ as your Savior and living daily for Him can you—"

"Thanks," said Wade, cutting me off. "I'll give it some thought."

But I knew he wouldn't.

I made Wade's situation a constant matter of prayer, asking the Lord to show me a way to open Wade's eyes to his need of Christ. Then, unexpectedly, it was Wade who came to *me*.

"Got a minute?" he asked, as I answered my front door one evening. "Can we talk somewhere in private?"

We found lounge chairs in my home office and sat down. Wade pulled a piece of paper from his shirt pocket, unfolded it, and passed it to me.

"That was in my pay envelope today," he explained. "It says the company is bringing in a line of robotic assembly units. This will help them downsize from 900 employees to 425."

"You lost your job?" I asked in amazement.

"No," he answered, "I was one of the lucky ones who had enough seniority in the union to be kept on. But it means the end to all the overtime I've been getting. And even worse, I'm being cut to thirty hours a week."

"But . . . that's *part-time* status, isn't it?"

He nodded. "It means my benefits package will be cut. I'll have to pay for my hospitalization myself, and they won't match me dollar for dollar any longer on my retirement fund. I'll have less money coming in but higher bills than ever."

"What're you going to do?"

Wade shrugged. "Nothin' else I *can* do but put ads in the paper and try to sell my motorcycle and boat and all that other stuff I've been buying the last couple of years. I never thought the company would treat me like this. I've worked hard for those people and now they act like they don't even know me. Man, this is the worst thing that could ever happen to me."

"No, you're wrong about that," I said gently, seeing an opportunity to make a point with Wade. "This will be rough on you, but you *are* a hard worker. You'll be able to find another part-time job to supplement your income. I know you. You'll survive."

Wade smiled weakly, trying to catch the fervor of my encouragement.

"Sure," I continued, "you'll survive this particular downsizing. But you won't survive the next one."

Wade's eyes narrowed and his forehead wrinkled. He stared questioningly at me.

"I've been telling you about how you need to secure your eternal salvation," I explained. "You've ignored me, thinking that your casual church attendance and your law-abiding life would be enough to get you into heaven. But it doesn't work that way. God does some downsizing of His own."

"Downsizing?" asked Wade, wondering if I was kidding with him. "What? In heaven?"

I reached to my desk and retrieved my Bible. I opened it to the book of Matthew.

"Listen to this, Wade," I said. "It's Jesus talking about people like you: 'Not everyone who says to Me, "Lord, Lord," will enter the kingdom of heaven; but he who does the will of My Father who is in heaven. . . . I will declare to them, "I never knew you; depart from Me, you who practice lawlessness"'" (7:21, 23 NASB).

"That . . . that's *me?*" Wade asked, gulping.

"It's the ultimate downsizing, Wade, and right now you're on the cut list."

"No!" he protested.

The loss of his full-time job status had made the downsizing illustration very real to him. He was scared, and rightfully so. I could see by his expression that he wanted help.

"There's time," I told him. "We can secure your place right now, this very minute, right here."

"Yeah, I . . . I want that," he stammered. "Will you help me?"

We bowed together and Wade asked Christ into his life. He prayed a sincere prayer and found salvation.

When we finished praying, Wade said, "I wish I would've done this before. This new security is better than a union, isn't it?"

I smiled and said, "It *is* a union, Wade: you and Christ, now and forever."

SCRIPTURE VERSES TO PONDER

"What should we do then?" the crowd asked. John answered, "The man with two tunics should share with him who has none, and the one who has food should do the same." Tax collectors also came to be baptized. "Teacher," they asked, "what should we do?" "Don't collect any more than you are required to," he told them. Then some soldiers asked him, "And what should we do?" He replied, "Don't extort money and don't accuse people falsely—be content with your pay."

—Luke 3:10–14

By the grace God has given me, I laid a foundation as an expert builder, and someone else is building on it. But each one should be careful how he builds. For no one can lay any foundation other than the one already laid, which is Jesus Christ. If any man builds on this foundation using gold, silver, costly stones, wood, hay or straw, his work will be shown for what it is, because the Day will bring it to light. It will be revealed with fire, and the fire will test the quality of each man's work. If what he has built survives, he will receive his reward. If it is burned up, he will suffer loss; he himself will be saved, but only as one escaping through the flames.

—1 Corinthians 3:10–15

QUESTIONS TO CONSIDER

1. Why do you think that witnessing to our neighbors and relatives and the people we work with is sometimes harder than talking to total strangers about the Lord?

2. In reading the newspapers and listening to radio and television news broadcasts, what current events do you feel are providing some opportunities for you to be a witness to someone else about how the Lord is in control of global events?

3. Have you or someone close to you experienced downsizing or a job loss for another reason? How does that impact your self-respect? How does it threaten your livelihood? How does it alter your plans for everything from planning vacations to deciding what to buy at the grocery store?

4. As Christians, we are told to care for the orphans and widows in our church. Does this imply that the church should be involved in social work? How can the church work in tandem with the government on assistance to the poor and needy, or even to those who are temporarily facing financial difficulties?

5. When things are going very well for us—financially, physically, educationally—do we tend to forget to give God the credit for such blessings? Why does that seem to be part of our human nature? How can we not fall into that trap?

SUGGESTED ADDITIONAL READING

Hensley, Dennis E. *How to Manage Your Money: Financial Strategies for Christians.* Anderson: Warner Press, 1989.

Hensley, Dennis E. *Money Wise: Honoring God with Creative Money Management.* Eugene, Ore.: Harvest House, 1991.

Sheets, Dutch. *How to Pray for Lost Loved Ones.* Detroit: Regal, 2002.

Sjogren, Steve. *Conspiracy of Kindness: A Refreshing New Approach to Sharing the Love of Jesus with Others.* Ann Arbor: Servant Publishers, 1993.

Sjogren, Steve. *Servant Warfare: How Kindness Conquers Spiritual Darkness.* Ann Arbor: Servant Publishers, 1996.

CHAPTER 13

THE UNEXPECTED BLESSING OF EXHAUSTION

Recently, a guest soloist at our church opened our evening service by singing the well-known gospel tune "Peace in the Valley." The man's slow phrasings and bass tones seemed to match the somber mood of the lyrics as he began, "Well, I'm tired and so weary. . . ."

This was a Sunday night, the end of a long week. As I looked around our sanctuary, I saw many an individual who seemed to be both tired and weary—some abnormally so. The vocalist's song only served to make these people slump even lower into their fatigue.

I recalled that D. L. Moody had once said that he was tired *in* the work of the Lord but not tired *of* the work. However, my fellow congregants that night seemed to be tired *of, in, on, around,* and *through* the work. They looked whipped.

I couldn't help but wonder how people who could sing, "There is joy in serving Jesus" one month, could now be so joy*less* and exhausted a month later. Even more to the point, I wondered how God could allow His servants to become so listless and worn out.

Oh, I knew that doctors could cite numerous reasons for fatigue— poor diet, stress, viruses, toxins, depression, sugar imbalance, lack of exercise, poor sleeping habits—but, to me, these people just seemed "bone weary."

A few days later the Lord used an object lesson to help me start thinking more deeply about the matter. My cordless phone went dead one morning during the middle of an important long distance business call. I hurried to another room, redialed the number on a standard wall phone, and was able to connect again to the party.

That afternoon I went to an electronics store to buy a replacement battery.

"You don't need a new battery," the clerk told me, after checking the battery I'd brought in.

"But it's dead," I insisted.

"No, it isn't," he said. "It's only discharged of its energy. Regular alkaline batteries for flashlights will go dead, but one of these new electronic batteries just runs down. If you drain all of the power from it the way you did, you can just let it sit idle for a day or two and then give it an electric recharging. You can go through three or four cycles like that before it needs to be replaced."

I found that hard to believe, but I decided to try it. (If it *did* work, I'd be saving five dollars.)

Well, sure enough, that clerk was right. I let the battery rest for two days. I then put it back in the phone one night and set it on electric recharge. By morning it was working just fine. It seemed contradictory; yet, in order to bring itself back to its full level of energy, the little battery first had to be totally run down and then allowed to do nothing for a while.

As I probed my Bible, I found identical situations with God's people; and, after giving it some thought, I was eventually able to come up with at least five reasons why this was probably so.

First, God can use exhaustion and weakness to remind us that our strength must come from Him and not our own resources. The apostle Paul suffered from a physical ailment which he prayed three times for God to heal. The healing was not granted, but greater grace was given to Paul to endure the problem. This left Paul still weakened by the condition and all the more dependent on God for his strength. This dependence kept Paul close to God. Thus, Paul could say, without irony, "When I am weak, then I am strong" (2 Cor. 12:10).

Second, God can use exhaustion to test, then reward our faith. After Peter had exhausted himself fishing all night and catching nothing, Jesus asked him to launch his boat again. He told Peter to cast out his nets. Peter explained to Jesus that he had already fished all night and the fish were just not there to catch. But, in faith, Peter added, "Nevertheless at thy word I will let down the net" (Luke 5:5 KJV). Peter cast his net. As a reward for his faithfulness, his nets began to haul in so many fish, they started to break and the boat nearly sank. It was an amazing blessing.

Third, exhaustion can serve as a reminder that we need to slow down and find some quiet time to be alone with God. Even Jesus did this. After preaching all day and feeding the five thousand, He sent the crowd home and told His disciples to go to the next town ahead of Him. He then "went up on the mountain by Himself to pray . . . alone" (Matt. 14:23 NASB). After having exhausted Himself and then taking time to recover, Jesus came back to walk on the water, calm the storm, and resume His preaching and healing. On numerous other occasions, Jesus separated Himself from everyone in order to rest and pray.

Fourth, God can use exhaustion to provide us with a new perspective on our lives. After Elijah had defeated the prophets of Baal and had outrun Ahab's chariot, he was spent of all his energy. He then heard that Jezebel had ordered him to be hunted down and killed. He ran out into the desert and collapsed. He begged God to let him die.

Elijah was discouraged, tired, hungry, scared, and lonely. He had never felt so drained of strength in his entire life. He longed for the ultimate rest—death! God, however, had much more need of Elijah's services, so He showed him in three different ways that things weren't nearly as bad as Elijah felt they were. God first granted Elijah a chance to sleep; following this, food and water were provided. These two steps—securing rest and nourishment—did much to revive Elijah's spirits.

The third step was the most crucial element of all, however. God told Elijah that he was not alone in his righteous stand. For a fact, there were seven thousand other people in that region who had refused to worship Baal (1 Kings 19:18). God was going to provide one of these seven thousand people to be a friend and helper to Elijah. Elisha became the student and companion of Elijah and "went after Elijah, and ministered unto him" (1 Kings 19:21 KJV). What Elijah had originally considered to be a crushing ordeal was really just the opening of a door to an entirely new opportunity to minister. It took sleep, food, and fellowship to help him gain this new perspective, however.

Fifth and final, a state of exhaustion can remind us of our present and future circumstances. In this life, man must "work by the sweat of his brow." Even in Christian service "the harvest is plenty but the laborers are few." In many ways, life on Earth is, indeed, laborious and exhausting. But it's also temporary. "There is no work . . . in the grave," Solomon wrote (Eccl. 9:10 KJV). Similarly, Jesus warned, "The night cometh, when no man can work" (John 9:4 KJV).

In the song "Peace in the Valley," the lyrics begin with a confession of weariness and weakness; they end with an optimistic look ahead to a day when "there'll be no sadness, no sorrow, no trouble . . . [just] peace in the valley for me." Our union with Christ, whether at our death or at His second coming, will begin this time of perpetual peace. As such, weariness *now* can serve to remind us of total rest *then*.

So it is then that exhaustion often proves to be a prelude to blessing. It can lead us to more dependence on the strength of God. It can test and reward our faith. It can draw us closer to God through prayer and meditation. It can provide new perspectives on the value of friendships with fellow believers. And it can turn our eyes toward our coming days in glory with the Lord.

So, the next time you feel bone weary and lethargic, just listen for your cell phone to ring. It'll remind you that *you* have a rechargeable battery, too.

SCRIPTURE VERSES TO PONDER

In the same way, the Spirit helps us in our weakness. We do not know what we ought to pray for, but the Spirit himself intercedes for us with groans that words cannot express. And he who searches our hearts knows the mind of the Spirit, because the Spirit intercedes for the saints in accordance with God's will.

—Romans 8:26–27

So will it be with the resurrection of the dead. The body that is sown is perishable, it is raised imperishable; it is sown in dishonor, it is raised in glory; it is sown in weakness, it is raised in power; it is sown a natural body, it is raised a spiritual body.

—1 Corinthians 15:42–44

I have labored and toiled and have often gone without sleep; I have known hunger and thirst and have often gone without food; I have been cold and naked. Besides everything else, I face daily the pressure of my concern for all the churches. Who is weak, and I do not feel weak? Who is led into sin, and I do not inwardly burn? If I must boast, I will boast of the things that show my weakness. The God and Father of the Lord Jesus, who is to be praised forever, knows that I am not lying.

—2 Corinthians 11:27–31

QUESTIONS TO CONSIDER

1. When is it that you feel you are weakest in your life—when you are physically worn out or when you are emotionally stressed? How does Satan use both of these weaknesses to try to lead us into depression, sin, and failure? What are some of the ways you can help yourself (or others) become spiritually revived during a time of weakness?

2. What special passages of Scripture do you turn to when you want to boost your confidence, rid yourself of the doldrums, or send a word of encouragement to a Christian friend?

3. Can you think back to a specific time in your life when you were physically ill or emotionally exhausted and it caused you to stop and totally reassess your life? If so, how did the Lord use that to help you get back on the right track? How did this seemingly terrible experience turn out to be something positive for your life in the long run?

4. How have such things as the fax machine, electronic mail, computers, palm pilots, cell phones, and microwave ovens seemed to make your life "faster" and more demanding than ever? Does it seem impossible to meet all the demands of modern life? How does our relationship with Christ provide a respite from all this chaos?

SUGGESTED ADDITIONAL READING

Barcus, Nancy. *Help Me, God, I'm a Working Mother!* Valley Forge, Pa.: Judson, 1982.

Hensley, Dennis E. *Positive Workaholism.* Indianapolis: R. and R. Newkirk, 1982.

Schuller, Robert. *Eight Words of Wisdom for Husbands and Wives.* Garden Grove, Calif.: Robert Schuller Ministries, 1987.

Stir, Virginia. *Peoplemaking.* Palo Alto, Calif.: Science and Behavior Books, 1972.

Swindoll, Charles. *Dropping Your Guard.* Waco, Tex.: Word, 1983.

Wilson, Sandra D. *Hurt People Hurt People: Hope and Healing for Yourself and Your Relationships.* Houston: Discovery House, 2002.

CHAPTER 14

PARDON ME FOR BEING BORING, BUT I CAME FROM A FUNCTIONAL FAMILY

Lately, whenever I find myself at a social gathering, I'm virtually at a loss for words. I have nothing to contribute to most conversations. You see, everyone else these days seems to have come from a dysfunctional family, or been in a codependent relationship, or suffered some sort of abuse. My "problem" is that I came from a functional family, I've never been codependent, and I've learned to cope with whatever bits of abuse life has dished out to me.

I keep wondering, *How can* everyone *be a victim?* Nobody admits to being at fault for anything these days. They're all just "victims of circumstances." People are doing atrocious things, but when they are called to account for their deeds, they all respond, "It's not my fault. *I'm* the *real* victim. I was emotionally abused."

While I would not discount the good work being done by organizations such as The Salvation Army, Alcoholics Anonymous, and other counseling and treatment programs, I think we need to shift from a negative to a positive approach to rehabilitation. We have developed a mind-set in this country wherein we all believe we have been abused in some way, and, therefore, none of us are accountable for our actions.

The "recovery movement" that has been so prevalent since 1975 has as its basis the need for people with a problem to make a public confession of their fallen condition: "Hello, I'm Sharon, and I'm an abusive mother." "Hello, I'm Ted, and I'm an alcoholic." "Hello, we're the Smiths, and we're chronic overeaters."

My own feeling is that if a person tells himself or herself a specific message enough times, that person will turn the message into a permanent identity. Tell yourself (and others) one hundred or two hundred times that you are an abusive mother and soon you probably *will* be.

I don't like that approach. I don't think that sort of negative reinforcement is what Jesus taught. He said for people to confess their sins one time (to God), repent of those sins, and then lead a *changed life* (Matt. 11:28–30; Eph. 4:22–24). Through Christ, the old nature can be set aside and we can "become new."

Rather than chanting, "I am the offspring of dysfunctional parents," we should proclaim, "I am a child of God" (Gal. 4:7; Phil. 2:15). Instead of moaning, "I'm just a victim," we should announce, "Through Christ, I am a *victor*" (Matt. 12:20; Eph. 5:8; 1 John 5:4). Instead of lamenting, "I am totally unworthy," we should remind ourselves, "I am redeemed and completely forgiven of my past sins" (Ps. 103:3; 1 John 1:9; Gal. 3:13–14).

Professional counseling and personal therapy can be productive. However, no one can become mentally or emotionally well until he or she deals with the sickness of the soul: *sin.*

By calling on Christ as Savior, accepting His plan of salvation, and truly believing that He will grant forgiveness, any one of us can become functional, productive, and happy.

Does this mean that everything this side of heaven will then be easy and worry free? No, definitely not. What it does mean, however, is that we will have a positive way of facing our dilemmas and coping with our trials. Jesus suffered, and so will we. But He was victorious over sin, and we can be, too.

When we learn to deal with the sin issue, it's amazing how much "healthier" we become.

SCRIPTURE VERSES TO PONDER

As Jesus was getting into the boat, the man who had been demon-possessed begged to go with him. Jesus did not let him, but said, "Go home to your family and tell them how much the Lord has done for you, and how he has had mercy on you." So the man went away and began to tell in the Decapolis how much Jesus had done for him.

—Mark 5:18–20

At that hour of the night the jailer took them and washed their wounds; then immediately he and all his family were baptized. The jailer brought them into his house and set a meal before them; he was filled with joy because he had come to believe in God—he and his whole family.

—Acts 16:33–34

He must manage his own family well and see that his children obey him with proper respect. (If anyone does not know how to manage his own family, how can he take care of God's church?)

—1 Timothy 3:4–5

If anyone does not provide for his relatives, and especially for his immediate family, he has denied the faith and is worse than an unbeliever.

—1 Timothy 5:8

QUESTIONS TO CONSIDER

1. Cain murdered his brother Abel. When asked about his brother's whereabouts, Cain answered, "Am I my brother's keeper?" Knowing that this event took place thousands of years ago, what does it tell us about the inherent disunity of most families?
2. What other families can you recall in the Bible wherein a lack of

proper training and discipline led to great problems? (Begin with Lot and his daughters. Also consider David and Absalom. Others?)

3. Paul commended Timothy's mother and grandmother for the way they educated him about the love of God and the obedience due Him. What other examples can you recall from the Bible wherein families did a good job of caring for their young ones by making them aware of God's teachings? (Begin with Noah and his sons. Also consider David and Solomon. Others?)

4. How have such things as television, public schools, motion pictures, magazines, and popular music gone about undermining our system of family values? What can we, as Christians, do to counterbalance this weight of antifamily sentiment?

5. What are some of the positive things you can recall about the way your parents brought you up? Have you been able to maintain similar patterns with your children?

SUGGESTED ADDITIONAL READING

Campbell, Ross. *How to Really Love Your Child.* New York: Signet Books, 1982.

Chesser, Barbara Russell. *Twenty-One Myths That Can Wreck Your Marriage.* Dallas: Word, 1990.

Dobson, James. *Hide or Seek: Self-Esteem for the Child.* Old Tappan, N.J.: Revell, 1974.

Fuller, Cheri. *Home-Life: The Key to Your Child's Success at School.* Tulsa, Okla.: Honor Books, 1988.

Garlett, Marti. *Who Will Be My Teacher?* Waco, Tex.: Word, 1985.

Perry, Jason, with Steve Keels. *You Are Not Your Own: Living Loud for God.* Nashville: Broadman & Holman, 2002.

CHAPTER 15

DOES GOD HAVE A
SENSE OF HUMOR?

The first time that I realized that the Bible was filled with comedy—and that most people weren't "getting" the jokes—was when I was a ten-year-old boy in a Sunday school class taught by Mrs. Bonnell. This was in Bay City, Michigan, in 1958, and we were studying the fourteenth chapter of Judges.

Mrs. Bonnell was saying, ". . . and it made Samson very angry that his friends had convinced his wife to tell them the answer to his riddle."

My head jerked up.

"Riddle?" I said out loud. "You're serious? This guy was cracking jokes with his pals? That's neat!"

Mrs. Bonnell frowned. "No!" she said emphatically. "Of course he was *not* cracking jokes. This is the Bible. It's a serious book. This *lesson* is serious. Samson was *testing* his companions."

I shook my head in disappointment. Rats! Too bad. To me, it would have been better the other way.

I recalled how just the previous Friday I had read a riddle on the side of a cereal box and how I couldn't wait to get to school so I could stump my friend John Humphrey with it. But it turned out that John had eaten the same cereal that morning, so he already knew the answer to the riddle. I was disappointed by that. It helped me identify with Samson's anger at having had his punch line taken away from him.

Mrs. Bonnell continued with the lesson, finishing chapter 14 and then approaching chapter 15 by first reading the entire text aloud. Because she wanted to protect our childish ears from words such as "jackass," she read from some sort of "children's" translation. When she got to verse 16, she read it aloud: "With a donkey's jawbone, I have made donkeys of them. With a donkey's jawbone, I have slain a thousand men."

As soon as I heard that, I roared with laughter.

All of the other children turned and looked at me, horror on their faces. One thing you *never* did in Mrs. Bonnell's class was to laugh at *anything* she read from the Bible.

As for me, I was holding my sides, doubled over in convulsions.

Mrs. Bonnell stopped reading.

"Dennis!" she snapped. "Stop that! How dare you!"

I looked at her, and in all sincerity said, "Don't—ha! ha!—you get it? It . . . it's a joke. It's funny."

My classmates' expressions switched from horror to curiosity. They looked to me for an explanation.

"It's a joke," I repeated. "He grabbed the jawbone of a donkey and bonked these guys so hard on their heads, they were as stupid as donkeys themselves. Get it? 'Blam!—you're a donkey!' 'Bonk!—so are you!' Bonk! Bonk! Blam! Blam!—donkeys piled up all over the place!"

Suddenly, the other kids *did* get it. And it *was* funny. And they started laughing, too, and all of us started saying, "Blam! Blam!" and, "Hee-haw, hee-haw . . . *bonk!*" And we were all laughing our sides out. I never had so much fun in a Sunday school class in my whole life.

Wow! That was hilarious. I loved it! I couldn't wait until the next Sunday rolled around. I mean, figure it out—if Samson was *this* funny, and he was just an athlete, why, the smart guys like Moses and Daniel and Solomon would probably annihilate us. This was going to be great!

When I got home, I told my dad the funny joke we'd heard in Sunday school. My dad was great. He really liked the joke. He laughed like crazy. His laughing made me start laughing all over again. It was a stitch. Then, my dad (who could remember every joke he'd ever heard, as well as every Bible story he'd ever read) did a bit of one-upsmanship. He found his Bible, opened it to Judges 15, and said, "There's more to the joke. You only heard *part* of it. It gets even funnier."

I stopped laughing and blinked in amazement.

"What?" I said, not quite following him. "What do you mean?"

"Look here," he said, pointing to verse 18. "After Samson killed a thousand men, he was dehydrated . . . totally exhausted . . . absolutely worn out. He needed some water. But there wasn't any. No water anywhere."

I looked concerned, not amused. My dad continued.

"So, here we see Samson just lift his arms and drop them to his sides. 'Oh, great,' he says. 'Here I just fought all afternoon and killed a thousand guys who wanted to slice me in half—I survived all that and now I'm going to die of thirst. Terrific! Just terrific! Can't a guy ever get a break, Lord?'"

I nodded my agreement. It did seem rather unfair.

"That's called irony," my dad explained. "Irony is another form of humor. It's like when something happens to you in life that is so unexpected or so unjust or so bizarre, you just have to laugh at it. It's not like 'tee-hee' funny, it's more like, 'Oh, man, how do I always manage to get myself into these crazy kinds of situations' funny."

I pondered that a second or two and then said, "Sort of like the stuff that happens to Lucy and Ethel on 'I Love Lucy.' Like that?"

He grinned broadly. "Yeah, yeah, exactly. It's that crazy kind of stuff that continually surprises you in life, where you've got to laugh or else go nuts."

"But . . . uh . . . well, did *God* think it was funny?" I asked, somewhat apprehensively, the stern visage of Mrs. Bonnell still fresh in my memory.

"God thought it was a scream," my dad assured me. "He totally agreed with poor Samson. He felt it was a bad deal, too, so He caused a little spring of water to flow out, and he let ol' Samson quench his thirst. Why, I bet they probably still look back on it today and have a good chuckle."

"So . . . there is some funny stuff in the Bible?" I asked.

"*Some! Some?*" my father responded gleefully. "Shucks fire, boy, the whole book is filled with marvelous pratfalls, jokes, one-liners, and funny stories. God instilled a sense of humor in all of us, and He wants us to use it. It keeps us healthy."

"Healthy?" I said, doing a double-take.

"Yes, healthy," he insisted. He flipped a few pages until he located Proverbs 17:22. "Listen to this: 'A merry heart doeth good like a medicine: but a broken spirit drieth the bones' [KJV]. That's advice from Solomon. He was the wisest man who ever lived, and he advised us to yuk it up."

"Really?" I said, looking at the verse myself. "Wow, Dad, that's cool. You're saying God enjoys jokes and funny stuff?"

"More than enjoys them," he answered, "He's one of the best practical jokers there ever was."

I looked stunned. "God *does* jokes?"

"Sure. Lots of them. Plenty of funny things."

"You're kidding. No way," I said. "Like what?"

"Well, for instance, one time he told a ninety-two-year-old woman named Sarah that she was going to have a baby. The woman laughed her head off when she heard that one. But the joke was on her. By the next month, she was pregnant. It got even funnier when she told her husband, because he was nearly one hundred at the time. But she *had* the baby, and when it was born, Sarah laughed all day. What a great joke this was on the people who told her she was too old to be a mom."

I smiled. "That's neat. I like that. Tell another one."

"Here's a favorite of mine," said my dad. "One time Jesus was at a wedding. They ran out of wine but the celebration was still going strong, so Jesus' mother asked him to change some water into wine. Jesus did it . . . but He made it so delicious, it shocked the people who first drank it. They weren't expecting something so tasty. It jolted them. I think that was the first 'spit-take' ever recorded in history."

My dad proceeded to act out the scene of an unsuspecting wedding guest nonchalantly taking a big swig of wine, then suddenly having his eyes bulge out, his cheeks puff, and his throat contract. It was a hoot. I made him do it six more times. We laughed until tears were rolling down our faces. This was grand fun.

"Tell another one," I begged.

"OK, one more," he consented, "but then you've got to do your own Bible reading. I don't want to give away all the surprises."

I nodded my agreement, but leaned forward for another story.

He proceeded to tell me the outrageously funny story of a man named Balaam who had a mule that could talk in Hebrew. The story took twenty minutes to tell, and every minute of it was a riot.

I pleaded for "just one more" story, so he told me about these crazy people who thought they could build a tower all the way up to heaven, and how one day God switched it so that the engineers were speaking Greek and the crew chiefs were speaking Egyptian and the carpenters were speaking Hebrew and the masons were speaking Latin and the teamsters hauling in the supplies were speaking Japanese and the cooks serving lunch were speaking Swedish. And, of course, it was the silliest situation I had ever heard of, and I was convulsed with laughter the whole time.

As he told this Tower of Babel story, my father acted out a ridiculous scene in which three men, all speaking different languages, were trying to explain the blueprints to each other ("No, no, we need to turn it *this* way. . . . Hey, you've got it upside down again!"). Then he did a routine in which a tapestry hanger, who spoke German, was trying to get his assistant, who spoke Spanish, to hand him the right tools ("Vat is dis vat you are handing me here, dumkoff! I zed I vanted un hammer, not mine luuuunch box!"). I laughed and applauded and begged for more.

We spent the whole day enjoying God's marvelous sense of humor. I also learned about all the various forms of humor: irony, surprise, puns, sight gags, repartee, double-meaning words, running jokes, clowning, misunderstandings, tricks, puzzles, humorous costumes, and riddles.

If there was a funny side to any story or lesson, my dad had the ability to see it. Every story he told was funnier than the one before.

I think my favorite was the story about Haman and Mordecai. I was convinced there couldn't be a funnier scene than what happened when the king asked Haman how he should reward a man for noble service to the kingdom. Thinking he meant himself, Haman said the king should dress this man in expensive clothes, put him on a mule, and have a member of the court walk through town leading this mule and calling out, "This is a man whom the king admires and loves and wishes everyone to honor." The king thought this was a marvelous idea, so he said to Haman, "The man I'm referring to is that old Jewish fellow Mordecai. Get him dressed . . . and then *you* can be the one to lead the mule throughout the town."

Oh, that was a marvelous surprise ending—worthy of O. Henry—and so wonderfully funny.

Despite the fact that I managed to encourage my dad to keep telling me funny stories from the Bible all afternoon, it turned out that he wasn't even able to scratch the surface of all the entertaining material that was in there. As he had said, the Book was just crammed with delicious examples of humor, each teaching a valuable lesson about how people interacted with others, how they thought, how they worked, and what God's plan was for their lives.

Mrs. Bonnell, bless her heart, had exposed me to the Bible, but she had not exposed me to God. My dad, on the other hand, had helped me enjoy God so much, I was motivated to want to spend more time in His Word. God had a sense of humor, there was no doubt about that. It was fun to explore His Word and to see the myriad of ways He chose to display His humor and to learn for what purposes He had used it.

As the years passed and I continued to study the Bible, I always looked for evidence of God's humor in situations. I became a Sunday school teacher at age twenty. At first, many of the people who attended came to my class out of habit or a sense of righteous obligation. As I exposed them to the humorous aspects of God's Word, the lessons took on a freshness and the people came out of enjoyment. Sunday school was fun. *God* was fun.

I remember telling the story of the twelve spies returning from

Canaan and giving their reports. Ten told scary tales of cities with great giants who made the Jews look like grasshoppers. I pointed out to my class that this was more than a little ludicrous.

"Here these spies were, standing at the bottom of the walls of Jericho, looking up sixty feet at a guard standing at his post," I would explain to my class. "A Jewish spy would yell up, 'Hey, Amalekite! How tall are you?' and the guard would yell back, 'I'm sixty-five feet, eight and a half inches tall. How tall are *you?*' The Jewish spy would yell back, 'About five-foot-six.' This would make the guard laugh, and he'd respond, 'You're a grasshopper compared to me. Here! Hold this anvil.' And then he'd drop something down from up there. Naturally, the Jews would run like crazy."

My class would get a good laugh out of this interpretation of the Canaan story. They knew, of course, that I was exaggerating. Nevertheless, it brought home the point that the spies had allowed their unsubstantiated fears to cloud their judgment. Because of this, they lost faith in God, refused to do what He commanded, and, consequently, had to be punished.

I've found that discovering the humorous aspects of Scripture can help people relate to the humanity of the folks who populate its pages. This, I believe, is what made Bill Cosby's routine about Noah so utterly hilarious in 1965. Cosby had God telling Noah to build the ark according to specific cubit lengths. Noah paused a moment, then responded, "What's a cubit?" This was funny because it was exactly what everyone listening to the routine was wondering, but it also was something *no one* would have *ever* had the nerve to ask about. Asking something so basic made Noah seem real to us.

Today, fortunately, we are seeing more elements of humor being used to make people think about such serious matters as salvation, redemption, witnessing, worshiping, and Bible study. I saw a bumper sticker recently that had a play on words based on the American Express credit card motto, "Don't leave home without it." The sticker read, "Jesus: Don't leave earth without Him." It made me smile, but it made its point.

I first started writing comedic stories based on biblical characters when I was in college. I wrote a story called "Noah and the Feminists," which speculated on what it would have been like trying to load the ark if the animals had been influenced by the women's liberation movement. When it was published, several people told me they found it very entertaining; but the shadow of Mrs. Bonnell fell over me, too, for there were others who felt that joshing and kibitzing had no place in religious matters and that I would be wiser to direct my creative energies elsewhere.

Back then, I disagreed with that. I still do. I've been teaching Sunday school to packed classes for more than thirty years, using humor as a teaching tool. God is immutable, unchanging. If He was funny when I was a kid, He still must be funny now. And as I continue to delve into His Word, I find this to be true.

I encourage people to pick up their Bibles, start smiling in expectation of having a good time, and then flip open the pages. I tell them to read and enjoy God's Word, and in the process, enjoy God.

By the way, did I ever tell you the story about the two Egyptian magicians who had this act in which they could turn rods into snakes? Well, it seems that these two guys—Jannes and Jambres were their names—were the hit of the royal court until one day this guy Moses walked in and . . .

SCRIPTURE VERSES TO PONDER

The LORD made the heavens.
Splendor and majesty are before him;
    strength and joy [are] in his dwelling place.
                        —1 Chronicles 16:26–27

And on that day they offered great sacrifices, rejoicing because God had given them great joy. The women and children also rejoiced. The sound of rejoicing in Jerusalem could be heard far away.
                        —Nehemiah 12:43

He prays to God and finds favor with him,
  he sees God's face and shouts for joy.

                            —Job 33:26

Then will I go to the altar of God,
  to God, my joy and my delight.
I will praise you with the harp,
  O God, my God.

                            —Psalm 43:4

Our mouths were filled with laughter,
  our tongues with songs of joy.
Then it was said among the nations,
  "The LORD has done great things for them."
The LORD has done great things for us,
  and we are filled with joy.

                        —Psalm 126:2–3

QUESTIONS TO CONSIDER

1. There is an old expression that says, "Laugh and the world laughs with you, weep and you weep alone." In what ways do you agree or disagree with this statement?

2. Norman Cousins wrote a series of articles and one book on the medical benefits of laughing as a pain reliever. The Bible had already explained this thousands of years earlier. Why do you think laughter is "like a good medicine"?

3. It takes three times as many facial muscles to form a frown as it does to form a smile. Why do you think God created us that way? What would seem to be His expectations of us as we go through life—our outlook? our countenance? our greetings to others? our attitudes?

4. Much of secular humor is based on ridicule of people, mocking specific individuals, debasing our government and political ser-

vants, and showing disrespect to parents. Surely this is not God's view of what is joyful and uplifting. Why does man pollute so much of what God has created for good?

5. A recent new ministry has been the advent of "Christian clowning." Can you think of other ways that humor can be used to share the gospel with those who have never heard the message of salvation?

SUGGESTED ADDITIONAL READING

Cooper, Darien. *You Can Be the Wife of a Happy Husband.* Wheaton: Victory Books, 1984.

Halter, Larry L. *Traits of a Happy Couple.* Waco, Tex.: Word, 1988.

Heavilin, Marilyn Willett. *Roses in December.* Nashville: Nelson, 1984.

MacDonald, Shari. *Humor for a Woman's Heart.* Nashville: Howard, 2002.

Seligson, M. *The Eternal Bliss Machine.* New York: Morrow, 1973.

Stinnett, Nick and John DeFrain. *Secrets of Strong Families.* New York: Signet Books, 1986.

CHAPTER 16

SOLVING THE MYSTERY
OF THE LIGHTED GOLD

Recently, something that had mystified me in the Bible for a long time was made clear. And the funny thing was, I discovered the answer while just relaxing on my vacation.

The mystery that had puzzled me was this: How will the city of New Jerusalem (Rev. 21–22), with its structure of pure gold, be able to project the great glow of light that prophesy says it will emit? The Bible says that God's glory will create an eternal shining light in the city, for He will dwell there. And it says that the city's walls will be made of jasper and that its twelve foundations will be made of twelve different kinds of precious stones.

But it also says that the city's pure gold is "like unto clear glass" (Rev. 21:18 KJV). Now, anyone who has looked at a nugget or a bar or even a bracelet of pure gold knows that there is nothing glasslike about it. Gold is solid, weighty, and opaque. Yet, those words remain in the Bible: "like unto clear glass."

I talked to some jewelers about "glassy gold," but none had ever heard of such a thing. The best they could surmise was that the Bible must have meant that the gold would be so highly polished, it would "reflect" light. But, no, that did not satisfy me. The Scriptures had called it "gold" that was "like unto clear glass." There had to be a way that that could be possible.

Two years later, never having come up with an acceptable interpretation or understanding of that passage in Revelation, I happened to be in Florida for a week of vacation with my wife. We drove to Winter Park for some shopping, and while there we strolled past the Morse Museum. Its outside posters noted that it housed original works of painting, sculpture, designer jewelry, and pottery. It also claimed to have one of the largest collections of glass windows, lampshades, and chandeliers designed and crafted by Louis Comfort Tiffany.

We entered and began to walk the hallways and rooms, enjoying the various displays. Suddenly, we chanced upon a gigantic mosaic comprised of two thousand separate pieces of stained glass and rare gems. It was called "The Butterfly Window," and it had been made in 1885 by Mr. Tiffany for the dining room of his home on 72nd Street in New York City.

The window captivated my wife and me for several reasons. From a distance it appeared to be a large, beautiful butterfly. However, as you drew nearer to it, you discovered that the outline and features of the giant butterfly actually were made up of hundreds and hundreds of smaller butterflies of every shape, size, and color imaginable. Its complexity of design and range of ingenuity were staggering.

"What an artist!" I said aloud. "This is the most phenomenal arrangement and balance of materials I've ever seen. No wonder he wanted to keep it for himself. It's astounding."

"Astounding, indeed," agreed a docent, who was standing nearby and had overheard my words. "But it is even more astounding than you yet know."

"Oh?" said my wife. "How's that?" The docent reached for a light switch on a nearby wall.

"Watch this," she said.

Slowly, she eased the dimmer switch from off to on . . . then to a brighter setting . . . then a still brighter setting . . . and finally to the brightest possible setting. As directional floodlights sent shafts of light through the window, the giant butterfly went through a kaleidoscopic metamorphosis. It evolved from deep, powerful purples to blood reds to hot oranges to flashy pinks. Absorbing blacks became soft grays, then muted silvers, then piercing, gleaming whites.

"That is how the sunlight entered Mr. Tiffany's kitchen each morning," announced the docent. "Every sunrise was a breathtaking, artistic masterpiece."

I stood there, genuinely awestruck. Not only were the thousands of pieces of glass electrifying the room with color, the framework and support lines were projecting the glowing, ever-expanding wash of liquid sunshine. It was this latter effect that mesmerized me most.

"How . . . how was he able to create the flowing sunshine?" I asked the docent. "I've never seen anything like it in my life."

She smiled in agreement.

"I understand your wonder," she said. "Many of Mr. Tiffany's secrets regarding how he glazed and fired and colored his glass were lost when he died. He kept no journals, and he was not a man to share his discoveries. However, we *do* know the secret of the 'flowing sunshine,' as you call it. Come closer, please."

My wife and I drew nearer, and the docent dimmed the floodlights.

"To create this effect, Mr. Tiffany pounded gold leaf on top of abalone shell," she explained, pointing to various places on the window. "The abalone shell was so fragile and the gold leaf was so thin, they both were transparent. However, they were *not* invisible. Light could pass through them, but not without diffusing itself through the off-white of the shell *and* the pure gold of the leaf layer. It made the gold look like clear glass. People have been enthralled by it for more than a century."

I stood still, so thrilled by this discovery, I couldn't say a word. I just kept staring at this "gold that was like clear glass."

The docent went away for a moment, then returned with a brochure. She underlined a passage, then passed it to me. I read it. "Paint," it said, "can imitate light. However, the colors coming from rare stones are light itself."

"That," said the docent, "was what made Tiffany's glass a work of art. Mr. Tiffany not only knew how to arrange gems and colored glass so that they displayed their greatest brilliance, he also found a way to make gold emit an array of light that would further magnify the stones' colors."

She paused a moment, looking at the Butterfly Window and losing herself for perhaps the thousandth time in its grandeur.

"It's marvelous, don't you think?" she said at last.

I nodded. "Heavenly," I concurred. "Absolutely heavenly."

SCRIPTURE VERSES TO PONDER

If you return to the Almighty, you will be restored:
   If you remove wickedness far from your tent
and assign your nuggets to the dust,
   your gold of Ophir to the rock in the ravines,
then the Almighty will be your gold,
   the choicest silver for you.

—Job 22:23–25

Because I love your commands
   more than gold, more than pure gold,
and because I consider all your precepts right,
   I hate every wrong path.

—Psalm 119:127–128

A good name is more desirable than great riches;
   to be esteemed is better than silver or gold.

—Proverbs 22:1

"The silver is mine and the gold is mine," declares the LORD Almighty.

—Haggai 2:8

The twelve gates were twelve pearls, each gate made with a single pearl. The great street of the city was of pure gold, like transparent glass.

—Revelation 21:21

QUESTIONS TO CONSIDER

1. When Jesus said, "I go to prepare a place for you," have you ever tried to imagine what your place in heaven will be like? Have you ever speculated on what heaven will be like? What sections of the Bible do you recall which offer descriptions of heaven and what our lives will be like there?

2. Knowing what we do about the glories of heaven, what does this imply about the sacrifice Christ had to make by leaving heaven even before He sacrificed Himself on the cross for us?

3. In this chapter we discovered one way that an artist used elements of nature to create something beautiful; in the process, he also provided an insight into biblical teachings. Have you ever encountered something in nature that has helped you better understand some passage in the Bible?

4. Besides experiencing the grandeur of heaven, what other aspects of a life in heaven are you looking forward to? Being with Jesus? Fellowshipping with the saints? Shedding your mortal body with all its frailties? What else?

5. How concerned are you that when you get to heaven, certain of your friends, neighbors, coworkers, relatives, and business associates might not be there because you never shared Christ with them? Are you concerned enough to do something about it?

SUGGESTED ADDITIONAL READING

Demaray, Donald E. *Laughter, Joy and Healing.* Grand Rapids: Baker, 1986.

Hayford, Jack W. *Worship His Majesty.* Ventura, Calif.: Regal, 2002.

Mains, David. *Full Circle.* Waco, Tex.: Word, 1971.

Sider, Ronald J. *Rich Christians in an Age of Hunger.* Downers Grove, Ill.: InterVarsity, 1977.

Yohn, Rick. *Discover Your Spiritual Gift and Use It.* Wheaton: Tyndale House, 1975.

CHAPTER 17

UNACCEPTABLE LOSSES

I was standing in an assembly area on a late September afternoon in 1971 during my tour of Vietnam. A colonel was on a raised platform addressing our company. He was praising us for the bravery and aggressiveness we had shown during a battle the week before.

My mind was wandering a bit. The sun was hot, I was tired, and, if the truth were known, I was more anxious to put the memory of that battle behind me than have someone remind me of it.

However, near the conclusion of the colonel's remarks, he said something that suddenly snapped me back to full attention.

"You men fought extremely well," the colonel said. "In fact, you fought so well, you routed the enemy in record time. We had projected a 15 percent casualty loss, but we only sustained an 8 percent loss. That was very acceptable. You are to be congratulated."

After we were dismissed, I stood in the same spot for several more minutes. I couldn't move. I had lost two good friends in that battle—guys I had bunked beside, eaten meals with, and worked alongside of for seven months—and the colonel had just referred to them as "acceptable" losses.

The loss of those men was not "acceptable" to me. I missed them. They were still very real to me. I knew the names of their wives and kids. I'd seen pictures of their parents, sisters, brothers, homes, cars. When I had cleaned out one of the men's locker two days earlier, I'd found a group photo of that man and me and four other guys in our company. Three of those men were now dead. I wasn't finding that situation to be the least bit "acceptable."

Military strategists had explained to us that all wars were wars of attrition: The army that could keep more soldiers in the field for a longer period of time would ultimately survive as the victor. As such, in any battle, the side that survived the fight losing the fewest number of men could be thought of as the side that had sustained "acceptable losses."

But, of course, that was the opinion of the *survivors*.

In the years that have passed since my stint in Vietnam, I have begun to wonder if there might be a parallel situation in the war against Satan.

For example, in a city of one hundred thousand people, there may be 125 churches. If these churches have successfully evangelized and led twenty thousand people to Christ, does that mean the other eighty thousand people who are bound for hell are "acceptable losses"?

If a family has two sets of grandparents, four uncles, six aunts, nine cousins, a dad, a mom, and five children, and twenty-one of these thirty family members know Christ as their Redeemer, are the other nine family members "acceptable losses"?

Surely from God's perspective, no soul is expendable or unimportant. As Peter explained, "The Lord . . . is patient toward you, not wishing for any to perish but for all to come to repentance" (2 Peter 3:9 NASB). One of the first verses children learn in Sunday school is John 3:16, which emphasizes to them "that *whosoever* believeth in him should *not* perish, but have everlasting life" (KJV; emphasis is author's).

This, then, should be a motivation for us to want to witness to others. It is God's will that *every person* in *every place* should one day come to know Him as Savior. No one *has* to be lost on the battlefield. It's a war, not of attrition, but of accumulation. The "victors" won't be those who kill people on the opposite side but, rather, those who help *save* others.

So, then . . . what are you waiting for?
Charge!

SCRIPTURE VERSES TO PONDER

Then Jesus told them this parable: "Suppose one of you has a hundred sheep and loses one of them. Does he not leave the ninety-nine in the open country and go after the lost sheep until he finds it? And when he finds it, he joyfully puts it on his shoulders and goes home. Then he calls his friends and neighbors together and says, 'Rejoice with me; I have found my lost sheep.' I tell you that in the same way there will be more rejoicing in heaven over one sinner who repents than over ninety-nine righteous persons who do not need to repent."

—Luke 15:3–7

The son said to him, "Father, I have sinned against heaven and against you. I am no longer worthy to be called your son." But the father said to his servants, "Quick! Bring the best robe and put it on him. Put a ring on his finger and sandals on his feet. Bring the fattened calf and kill it. Let's have a feast and celebrate. For this son of mine was dead and is alive again; he was lost and is found." So they began to celebrate.

—Luke 15:21–24

QUESTIONS TO CONSIDER

1. When you started to grow up and your parents told you it was time to give your childhood toys and games to charity, did you feel a pang of nostalgia? Why were you reluctant to give away these ties to your past? In what way does this parallel a situation of how we will have to be separated from many of our loved ones who won't be in heaven because they did not profess Christ

as Savior? How will this latter situation be much worse? What can be done now to avoid such separation and pain?

2. Have you ever been far away from your family for a long time, perhaps as an exchange student in a foreign country or away in military service or transferred because of a business assignment? Despite the distance, in what ways did you know that you were not emotionally separated from your family and close friends? In what ways does Christ remind us that we can never be separated from Him? How can we go about sharing this relationship with people we meet in life?

3. If a home burns down, it can be rebuilt. If a car is wrecked, a new one can be purchased. How is it different with the loss of a loved one? How should knowing such a difference motivate us to see that, even in death, we would only be separated a short while from those we love?

SUGGESTED ADDITIONAL READING

Cook, Jerry. *Love, Acceptance and Forgiveness.* Ventura, Calif.: Regal, 1979.

Hensley, Dennis E. *How to Fulfill Your Potential.* Anderson, Ind.: Warner Press, 1989.

Little, Paul. *How to Give Away Your Faith.* Downers Grove, Ill.: InterVarsity, 1966.

Morris, David. *A Lifestyle of Worship.* Ventura, Calif.: Regal, 2002.

Ortiz, Juan. *Cry of the Human Heart.* Carol Stream, Ill.: Creation House, 1977.

Scazzero, Pete. *Introducing Jesus.* Downers Grove, Ill.: InterVarsity, 1991.

CHAPTER 18

A MAJORITY OF ONE

Years ago, when my children were still young, I took a job in a public relations department at a college. I had a great deal of freedom to come and go as I pleased. As long as I achieved the desired results, no one monitored my activities.

However, despite not having anyone to hold me accountable for my comings and goings, it seemed that the Holy Spirit made me very conscious of any weaknesses in my work habits. For example, if I arrived a few minutes late at my office in the morning or after lunch, I'd experience a terrible sense of guilt; it caused me to work late at the end of the day to compensate. Or, if I took someone to lunch to discuss college-related matters, I'd feel uneasy if the bill seemed too high for my expense account; so, I'd wind up paying for my own lunch out of my personal money.

Part of me resented the way I *always* was made to feel self-conscious about these situations. No one else in my department seemed to worry over such matters. My colleagues came in late and didn't make up the lost time. They charged *all* of their expenses to their entertainment accounts without batting an eye.

"Why is it just *me*, Lord?" I wondered. "Why doesn't everyone else feel honor bound to do what's right? Why is it that the Holy Spirit just seems to be focusing on *me?*"

After several weeks of complaining like this, I received an answer from God. It came by way of a real-life illustration.

One Saturday afternoon my seven-year-old son came running into the house. He was all excited.

"Dad, the other kids are riding their bikes over to the park on the other side of town," he told me. "I want to go with them. Is it OK?"

I grimaced and shook my head. "Sorry, pal, but that's too far for a little guy like you to go by bicycle. I'll drive you over in the car, though. You can meet your friends there."

"No," he protested with a whine. "We want to go on our bikes. Come on, Dad, I'll be careful. It'll be fun. Please, Dad?"

I smiled consolingly. "Not until you're older, son. There are a lot of streets to cross between here and the park, and lots of busy traffic. I'd worry too much about you. Come on. We can put your bike in the trunk and you can ride it once you get to the park."

He stamped his foot in anger. "You never let me have any fun," he said loudly. "Mike's dad is letting him ride his bike and so is Allen's dad and Stuart's dad and Joey's dad. Everybody else is getting to ride a bike. Why not me?"

"Look," I said flatly, "I don't care *how many* other kids are riding bikes to the park. I still say it's too dangerous for you and you aren't going to do it. I love you, and I want what's best for you. Now, you can either go over in the car or else stay here."

After another ten minutes of railing against my unfairness (and getting nowhere), he finally gave up and let me drive him to the park. He sulked the whole way.

When we arrived, the other kids gathered around our car.

"Didn't Stuart come with you?" they all asked.

"No," I answered. "Was he supposed to?"

"Well . . . no, not really," said one of the older boys, "but he never showed up. We sort of outdistanced him a few blocks after we left home. We thought he probably went back to his house or to your place."

I felt sudden concern. "You mean you lost him?" I asked. "You left little Stuart all by himself?"

"We thought he knew the way," said another boy, looking down at his shoes.

"Quick! All of you! Into my car! Show me where you left him."

We drove back to the street where the group had left Stuart. He wasn't around. We went to a gas station and called our house and Stuart's. He hadn't been to either place. Stuart's parents drove to our location to join our search. Everyone was becoming very concerned by now.

Fortunately, an hour later, we located Stuart. He was sitting in an alley, dirty and crying. His bicycle chain had snapped after he'd been abandoned. He'd tried to find his way back home, but he'd gotten lost.

After Stuart and his bike were both safe at home again, I thought it would be a good time to emphasize to my son how right I had been in not letting him go off on his bike with the other boys. But before I could begin my fatherly lecture, my words caught in my throat.

I suddenly remembered what I had said to my son earlier that day about how I hadn't cared about *how many other people* were doing something I felt wasn't right or good for him. That was *exactly* how my heavenly Father had been treating me!

No matter how many other people had been taking advantage of my employer, God had refused to let me be part of such behavior. I had been griping and whining about how "unfair" it all was, but God had not been swayed by my childish pouting and complaining. He had held firm to what was right and best for me. Now, I was able to see that.

I recalled how in Revelation 3:19 Jesus said, "Those whom I love, I reprove and discipline" (NASB).

I put my arm around my boy and said, "We've *both* learned a good lesson today, son."

SCRIPTURE VERSES TO PONDER

For you are a people holy to the LORD your God. The LORD your God has chosen you out of all the peoples on the face of the earth to be his people, his treasured possession.

—Deuteronomy 7:6

But if serving the LORD seems undesirable to you, then choose
for yourselves this day whom you will serve, whether the gods
your forefathers served beyond the River, or the gods of the
Amorites, in whose land you are living. But as for me and my
household, we will serve the LORD.

—Joshua 24:15

But you are a chosen people, a royal priesthood, a holy nation, a people belonging to God, that you may declare the
praises of him who called you out of darkness into his wonderful light. Once you were not a people, but now you are the
people of God; once you had not received mercy, but now
you have received mercy. Dear friends, I urge you, as aliens
and strangers in this world, to abstain from sinful desires,
which war against your soul.

—1 Peter 2:9–11

QUESTIONS TO CONSIDER

1. Can you remember being in school when you had to be up on all
   the latest trends and dressed in the most current fashions? Social
   scientists call this the "herd instinct." We don't want to feel out of
   place. Knowing this about human nature, what problems does
   this present when we feel we need to maintain our testimony when
   the crowd wants us to go or behave in another way?

2. What incidents from the Bible can you recall wherein one saint
   of the Lord had to stand alone against the masses? Begin by
   considering Noah, Job, Daniel, and Esther.

3. Without seeming to be a rabble-rouser, how can you make a
   stand for the Lord at work? in your neighborhood? among your
   social acquaintances?

4. Think for a moment of some recent situations in which you
   have taken a stand for the Lord by your actions or words or
   decisions. In what ways were you ostracized or criticized for

this stand? How did you find strength through the Scriptures or prayer to enable you to hold to your convictions?

5. Does Satan also have his followers who are willing to take a stand for evil? What motivates them? To what ends should we, as Christians, go to resist their efforts to alter our government, our schools, our way of life?

SUGGESTED ADDITIONAL READING

Anderson, James D. *To Come Alive.* New York: Harper and Row, 1973.

Barnes, Bob. *Fifteen Minutes Alone with God, for Men.* Eugene, Ore.: Harvest House, 1995.

Belew, M. Wendell. *Churches and How They Grow.* Nashville: Broadman & Holman, 1971.

Bridges, Jerry. *I Exalt You, O God.* Colorado Springs: WaterBrook, 2002.

Hunt, June. *Seeing Yourself Through God's Eyes.* Grand Rapids: Zondervan, 1989.

Weber, Stu. *Tender Warrior.* Sisters, Ore.: Multnomah, 1993.

CHAPTER 19

JUST A MINUTE OF
YOUR TIME

According to *Financial Worth* magazine, the most successful stock and bond portfolio manager in 1993 earned *for himself* $1.1 billion in salary, commissions, and bonuses. This man invested monumental amounts of money on behalf of an elite clientele of wealthy individuals and corporations.

Assuming that this man worked a forty-hour work week and only took the standard two weeks of vacation time, his consultation fee would be $550,000 per hour (40 hours x 50 weeks = 2,000 hours; $1.1 billion divided by 2,000 hours = $550,000 per hour).

Many people don't make that kind of money in an entire lifetime; yet, here is a man who earns $550,000 per hour, *every working hour of the year!*

Now, with that in mind, think of how humorous some of our day-to-day catch phrases would sound if they were applied to this man.

"Uh, excuse me, friend, but can I have a minute of your time?" you might ask.

"That depends," the investor would reply, "on whether or not you have $9,167 you can spare."

Or how about, "Wait a second, just wait a second, while I explain this," to which the investor would respond, "OK, but it'll cost you $152.78 for every second you hold me here."

Talk about the expression "time is money"—this fellow was the walking epitome of that.

So, knowing how valuable this gentleman's time was, you would never just expect to walk into his office and sit down and have a chat for an hour or so. That would be unthinkable. No doubt this man was a very gracious and generous person, but the demands on his time were unrelenting. After all, he had not become such a highly successful consultant by wasting time.

If by chance, however, this man *were* to have granted you a few moments of his time to discuss a personal need of yours, you would, without a doubt, have felt tremendously grateful. You would have been so overwhelmed by this unselfish act of generosity and kindness, you would never have been able to express your gratitude adequately.

Let's now take this to an even higher level of time value.

Think of the scene of the crucifixion of Christ.

There was Jesus, spikes driven into His hands and feet, a wreath of thorns piercing His forehead and scalp. He was wearing virtually no clothes despite a blazing Middle East sun overhead, and He had been given no water for hours. People were mocking Him. His mother was grieving at the foot of His cross. Soldiers were gambling for His robe. A man on another cross nearby was taunting Him and denouncing His deity.

Atop all these physical and emotional torments, Jesus was also carrying the sin debt of the world. Every act of murder, theft, rape, deception, lying, drunkenness, abuse, and blasphemy ever committed, or yet to be committed, was put on Him for purification and atonement.

The overall pressures and demands on Jesus at this point, both humanly and spiritually, were beyond all our abilities to comprehend.

And yet . . .

Amid all this agony, a lone voice asked, "Excuse me, Lord . . . but have you got a minute?"

On yet a third cross was another man. This man was a criminal, someone who openly admitted to being guilty and publicly acknowledged that he deserved the punishment he was receiving. But he was repentant. And he didn't want to die knowing that he would face an even worse judgment in the next life.

His only hope for redemption was a word of forgiveness and pardon from the beaten and tortured individual who hung next to him. But how could he dare ask *anything* of someone in such a wretched state? The thorns . . . the spikes . . . the sun. It would be a miracle if He could even hear him, much less respond.

And even if He *did* hear, why should He waste his precious time on a worthless thief? Surely He had much weightier matters to contend with, to cope with, to focus on.

And yet . . .

And yet, this was the sinful man's only chance to be pardoned. He would *have* to ask for a moment of this Savior's time.

"Lord, remember me when you come into your kingdom," he pleaded earnestly.

Slowly, ever so slowly, the weary head of the Savior lifted. The eyes turned lovingly on the desperate petitioner. There was no malice in the expression, no stern gaze of admonition. Instead, the look revealed a recognition of the sincerity of the sinner's repentance. A pardon would be granted. Forgiveness would be bestowed.

"This day," responded the Savior, "you shall be with me in Glory."

The minute then passed. The Great Man had found the time to help the lost sinner. Despite all the demands on Him, He hadn't been too busy to hear a cry for help and to respond to it.

Today, He's still listening . . .

And He's still responding.

If you don't believe me, *take a minute.* Find out for yourself.

SCRIPTURE VERSES TO PONDER

There is a time for everything,
and a season for every activity under heaven:

a time to be born and a time to die,
a time to plant and a time to uproot,
a time to kill and a time to heal,
a time to tear down and a time to build,
a time to weep and a time to laugh,
a time to mourn and a time to dance,
a time to scatter stones and a time to gather them,
a time to embrace and a time to refrain,
a time to search and a time to give up,
a time to keep and a time to throw away,
a time to tear and a time to mend,
a time to be silent and a time to speak,
a time to love and a time to hate,
a time for war and a time for peace.

—Ecclesiastes 3:1–8

For it is time to seek the LORD, until he comes and showers righteousness on you.

—Hosea 10:12

What I mean, brothers, is that the time is short. From now on those who have wives should live as if they had none; those who mourn, as if they did not; those who are happy, as if they were not; those who buy something, as if it were not theirs to keep; those who use the things of the world, as if not engrossed in them. For this world in its present form is passing away.

—1 Corinthians 7:29–31

QUESTIONS TO CONSIDER

1. In *Alice in Wonderland* the White Rabbit was always running around yelling, "I'm late, I'm late, for a very important date," yet he had no idea where he was supposed to be or for what reason. Do you ever find yourself in a similar situation? Do you ever get

so caught up in your job and career that you forget that your family, your Christian brothers and sisters, and your own needs require some special attention? If so, what do you think you can start doing about that?

2. Have you ever looked into a casket and said, "I meant to call this person and tell her how much I loved her"? Have you ever read an obituary and thought, *I was always going to get out there to the rest home and visit him*? What can you do *today* to see to it that the time of your life is invested more in the people who have meant a lot to you?

3. Have you ever seen a little sign that reads: "Only one life, 'twill soon be past; only what's done for God will last"? Do you feel that is true? If so, what should you be doing about it?

4. If you knew for certain that the Lord would be returning this next Saturday morning, how would you use this week's time? In what ways should you be using your time that way anyway?

SUGGESTED ADDITIONAL READING

Engstrom, Ted W., and Alex R. MacKenzie. *Managing Your Time: Practical Guidelines on the Effective Use of Time.* Grand Rapids: Zondervan, 1967.

Hensley, Dennis E. *How to Manage Your Time: Time Management Strategies for Active Christians.* Anderson, Ind.: Warner Press, 1989. Translated into Russian, Source of Life Publishers, Russia, 1997.

Hensley, Dennis E. *Staying Ahead of Time: How to Make Time Management a Way of Life . . . And Why It's Worth It!* Indianapolis: Bobbs-Merrill, 1981.

Hummel, Charles. *Tyranny of the Urgent.* Downers Grove, Ill.: InterVarsity, 1967.

Mains, David. *Full Circle.* Waco, Tex.: Word, 1971.

Warden, Michael D. *Experience God in Worship.* Loveland, Colo.: Group, 2002.

CHAPTER 20

I NEVER KNEW YOU

Most folks are familiar with the passage in Matthew 7:21–23 in which Jesus spoke about people who would be turned away from the kingdom of heaven. Jesus predicted that certain folks would demand entrance into heaven based on the fact that they claimed to have a relationship with God.

Jesus explained, however, that only people who had been redeemed through a personal salvation experience with Christ would be admitted into heaven. He noted that many people would be shocked when they were turned away from heaven's gate.

A few years ago, some people in Georgia discovered just how much of a shock this really was going to be.

During one summer in which President George Bush Sr. was in the White House, he and his wife decided to take a short vacation on St. Simon's Island. The President and Mrs. Bush had honeymooned at this lovely Georgia resort area in 1945 and now wanted to go back again. Arrangements were made for them to stay at a five-star hotel, and they arrived with a full entourage of reporters, secretaries, administrative aides, chauffeurs, and, of course, Secret Service agents.

Mrs. Barbara Bush asked if the quaint little historic Christ's Church was still in operation on the island, and she was told that it had not missed a Sunday service in more than 225 years. John and Charles Wesley had visited the island when it was a colonial outpost, and they had preached under trees that still stood on the church grounds. The original stained glass windows had been brought from Germany and had been installed before the Civil War, and in the early 1900s, Louis Comfort Tiffany himself had created a stained glass window for this church. This news delighted the First Lady. She decided that she and the President would worship there next Sunday.

When word got out throughout the community that the President and First Lady were going to be in attendance at Christ's Church on Sunday, literally hundreds of island residents decided to attend that service, too. On Sunday, when the Secret Service agents arrived early to secure the church for the President's safety, they found the sidewalks, garden areas, and yards all overrun with crowds of people waiting for the church doors to open so they could rush inside.

The security agents were dumbfounded. There was no way they could search all of these people, much less run clearance checks on all of them. But who knew what sorts of cranks or misfits might be mingling with the legitimate local citizens? It was a security nightmare, and the agents could think of no way to cope with it.

Soon, the time drew near for the President's limousine to arrive. Something had to be done, and fast!

The chief of security dashed to the pastor's office and led him by the arm to the front door.

"OK, here's what we're going to do," the agent announced. "We're going to unlock the door and have you step outside onto the porch. You'll scan the crowd. Whenever you see the faces of people you recognize as faithful members of this church—the folks who show up every week—we'll have you point out those people to my men. The agents will then escort those folks through the crowd and into the church."

The pastor couldn't help but smile. Oh, my, this was going to be interesting.

The two men walked out. One by one the pastor began to acknowledge faces.

"Yes, those folks are the Johnsons," he said. "Bring them inside. Oh, and there are the Smiths and the O'Brians and the Winslows. Let them in, too. And over there . . . those folks are the Vanderkemps . . . and back there I see the McMillans and their children. . . ."

As the pastor identified the members, hundreds of other people called out, "Here! Look here! I've been a resident on this island for years! Choose me! Choose me!"

But the pastor, with a regretful shrug of his shoulders, only responded, "I'm sorry. I can't ever remember seeing you before. I'm afraid I have to say no."

It didn't take long for the tiny church to fill. The President and Mrs. Bush arrived and were brought in the back way. All doors and windows were then locked tightly. Bodyguards stood at each entrance, barring admission to anyone not previously chosen.

"Hey! We want to go inside, too," the people called out. "Open the doors. Let us in."

But the bodyguards remained immovable. And the doors behind them stayed locked.

A week later, these words from Jesus were printed on the back of the Christ's Church bulletin:

> Not every one that saith unto me, Lord, Lord, shall enter into the kingdom of heaven; but he that doeth the will of my Father which is in heaven. Many will say to me in that day, Lord, Lord, have we not prophesied in thy name? and in thy name have cast out devils? and in thy name done many wonderful works? And then I will profess unto them, I never knew you: depart from me (Matthew 7:21–23 KJV).

SCRIPTURE VERSES TO PONDER

> He said to them, "Go into all the world and preach the good news to all creation. Whoever believes and is baptized will be saved, but whoever does not believe will be condemned."
> —Mark 16:15

This is the meaning of the parable: The seed is the word of God. Those along the path are the ones who hear, and then the devil comes and takes away the word from their hearts, so that they may not believe and be saved. Those on the rock are the ones who receive the word with joy when they hear it, but they have no root. They believe for a while, but in the time of testing they fall away.

—Luke 8:11–13

Now, brothers, I want to remind you of the gospel I preached to you, which you received and on which you have taken your stand. By this gospel you are saved, if you hold firmly to the word I preached to you. Otherwise, you have believed in vain.

—1 Corinthians 15:1–2

Now we know that if the earthly tent we live in is destroyed, we have a building from God, an eternal house in heaven, not built by human hands.

—2 Corinthians 5:1

QUESTIONS TO CONSIDER

1. In what ways do some people make "an appearance" of being righteous, yet actually remain *transparent* to everyone around them?
2. Jonah, Job, Peter, Thomas, and other biblical personages showed weakness of faith. How is this different from false piety?
3. If a person is a "token" or "showcase" Christian, how will he or she be false in other aspects of life (on the job? in the family? as a citizen?)?
4. The expression "coattail Christians" is sometimes used to refer to second generation offspring who rely on their parents' and grandparents' religious faithfulness to hold them in good stead with God. What is obviously wrong with this sort of thinking?

5. In what ways have aspects of your Christian testimony become more "show" than "go," more "flair" than "care," and more "talk" than "walk"?

SUGGESTED ADDITIONAL READING

Brand, Paul, and Philip Yancey. *In His Image.* Grand Rapids: Zondervan, 1984.

Jackson, Dave and Neta. *Living Together in a World Falling Apart.* Carol Stream, Ill.: Creation House, 1974.

Lewis, C. S. *Beyond Personality.* New York: Macmillan, 1952.

Myers, Ruth, with Warren Myers. *Thirty-One Days of Praise.* Sisters, Ore.: Multnomah, 2002.

Thurman, Chris. *If Christ Were Your Counselor.* Nashville: Nelson, 1993.

CHAPTER 21

THE PREPARED BUT UNUSED PLACE

An elderly widow in our church asked me if I would drive her to the cemetery one afternoon so that she could tend to the grave site of her late husband. When we arrived, I decided to give her some private time with her memories. I left her at her family plot and told her that I would take a walk and be back in half an hour.

I strolled among the tombstones, reading dates and memorial messages. It was midafternoon of a weekday, so the graveyard was virtually empty except for me and one lone groundskeeper pruning some hedges.

Suddenly, I came upon a special area enclosed with a low wrought-iron fence. A pink and blue marker near the entrance gate was labeled "Babyland." I'd never seen this part of the cemetery before. Here was a separate area just for the burial of infants.

I pulled the gate open and went inside, among the small graves and miniature headstones. I glanced at the chiseled messages all around me: "Little Timmy, Three Weeks of Happiness in Our Lives" . . . "Our Lovely Baby Caroline, Gone but Always Loved" . . . "Sarah and Cindy, Twin Joys" . . . "Bobby, Our Hearts' Delight" . . . and so on.

Instinctively, I found myself pulling out my wallet and flipping to the photos of my son and daughter, both now in their late twenties and both alive and healthy. It was comforting to see their faces. Losing either one of them would be like tearing my heart out. I could only imagine the agony the parents of these lost children around me must have gone through.

"Shakes you a bit, doesn't it?" a voice said behind me.

I turned around quickly. It was the groundskeeper, his hedge clippers still in hand.

"Uh, yeah . . . yes, it does," I admitted. I replaced my wallet and stood there a little self-conscious.

"Come here," said the man. "I'll show you something even more emotional." He walked past me, turned left, and went to the side of a small grassy embankment. I followed mutely.

"Here!" he said pointing. "These are new graves, all dug within the past three months. Look at them."

I scanned the area before us and I was amazed. Here, like in the other section of Babyland, were short graves and small tombstones. But in addition to that, the graves were covered with baby rattles, teething rings, little bibs with cartoon characters, dolls, stuffed animals, storybooks, booties and tiny caps, baby bottles, pacifiers, teddy bears, and bunting blankets.

"What is all this?" I asked.

"Treasures," answered the groundskeeper. "These couples spent nine months fixing up a nursery, attending baby showers, buying toys and a crib and diaper bags. Their whole lives were focused on the arrival of a baby. They had the room all decorated and filled with everything a baby could want or need. Then, at last, the wonderful day came: the baby was born."

He paused a moment.

"And then it died," he added, softly.

I bent down slowly, gently touching some of the items.

"People who've spent so much time thinking about the arrival of a new life are totally caught off-guard by sudden death," the man continued. "They don't know what to do. These things you see all around you were supposed to be for the new babies . . . so the parents, in their confusion and grief, go ahead and bring them here to their babies. To us it may seem irrational, but to the parents it's a way of fulfilling a promise to their child."

I stood up and stepped back a couple of paces.

"I don't like it here," I said. "The sadness of this place is too real. I'm a parent myself. My wife and I have two kids, both older now but still very close to us."

The man nodded. "Me, too. We've got three. This place gets to me, too. I'll walk you out."

We turned, but then I stopped abruptly.

"Are you a Christian?" I asked the man.

"Yes," he said, "I am."

"Something just occurred to me," I told him. "Do you remember what Jesus said to His disciples during the last supper? He told them, 'In My Father's house are many dwelling places . . . I go to prepare a place for you.'"

"Yes, I know that passage," said the groundskeeper.

"Well, as sad as this little graveyard is," I said, continuing, "imagine what it must be like for Christ. He wants to prepare special rooms for *all* of His children so that one day they can come and live with Him. He's the anxious and eager parent. . . ."

The groundskeeper broke in, ". . . *but,* some children will die."

I nodded. "Yes. They'll die and will never enter into their Father's house. How sad. How terribly, terribly sad. Just like these little babies."

"No," said the man, "not exactly the same." He pointed to a tombstone upon which a Bible verse was carved: "Believe in the Lord Jesus, and you shall be saved" (Acts 16:31).

"These babies are already with the Father. That was *His* decision. For the others, however, the decision is theirs."

I weighed that mentally for a moment, looked back at the little grave sites, and then back at the groundskeeper.

"You're right."

We closed the gate behind us as we left.

SCRIPTURE VERSES TO PONDER

At that time the sign of the Son of Man will appear in the sky, and all the nations of the earth will mourn. They will see the Son of Man coming on the clouds of the sky, with power and great glory. And he will send his angels with a loud trumpet call, and they will gather his elect from the four winds, from one end of the heavens to the other.

—Matthew 24:30–31

Do not let your hearts be troubled. Trust in God; trust also in me. In my Father's house are many rooms; if it were not so, I would have told you. I am going there to prepare a place for you. And if I go and prepare a place for you, I will come back and take you to be with me that you also may be where I am. You know the way to the place where I am going.

—John 14:1–4

But our citizenship is in heaven. And we eagerly await a Savior from there, the Lord Jesus Christ, who, by the power that enables him to bring everything under his control, will transform our lowly bodies so that they will be like his glorious body.

—Philippians 3:20–21

QUESTIONS TO CONSIDER

1. Have you ever attended the funeral of a baby or a very young child? Were the child's parents Christians or non-Christians? How did this make a difference in the way you tried to comfort the parents (and siblings) of the dead child?
2. Think of people in the Bible who lost children (King David, Rizpah, etc.). How did they react? In what ways did they turn to God for comfort and understanding of these losses? How did such losses alter their lives?

3. One woman who lost two children to drunk drivers retaliated by forming a national organization known as M.A.D.D. (Mothers Against Drunk Driving). Can it be that God can even use the death of a child to redirect our lives? In what ways has even an illness your child has suffered caused you to see things in a new light?

4. Many mothers and fathers have lost grown children during a time of war. Some have accepted this loss, knowing that the young man or woman chose to risk his or her life for a greater cause. Still, the sacrifice and sense of loss are grievous. In light of this, what should be our feelings about the sacrifice of Christ, who died in our place that we might be made pure?

SUGGESTED ADDITIONAL READING

Cranford, Clyde. *Because We Love Him: Embracing a Life of Holiness.* Sisters, Ore.: Multnomah, 2002.

Glenn, H. Stephens, and Jane Nelson. *Raising Self-Reliant Children in a Self-Indulgent World.* Rockland, Calif.: Prima, 1989.

Hybels, Bill. *Laws That Liberate.* Wheaton, Ill.: Victor Books, 1985.

Lewis, C. S. *Mere Christianity.* New York: Macmillan, 1943.

Lewis, Paul. *Forty Ways to Teach Your Child Values.* Wheaton: Tyndale House, 1988.

Schaeffer, Francis. *How Should We Then Live?* Old Tappan, N.J.: Revell, 1976.

CHAPTER 22

THE POWER OF SUBTLE ACTIONS

It was a subtle, but very reassuring gesture.

I was scheduled for knee surgery in two hours and the surgeon who was going to perform the operation came by my room to shave my knee.

At first, this baffled me. With so many nurses and orderlies around, why would a surgeon perform so menial an act as shaving my knee?

Then it dawned on me.

He wants me to be assured that he knows which leg needs the operation.

I smiled . . . and relaxed. This guy must have taken a course or two in psychology.

Jesus, too, used subtle actions as ways of reassuring, teaching, and helping people. We can benefit greatly by emulating His subtle ways.

THE SUBTLE POWER OF SILENCE

Jesus was not one to scream, wail, or gnash teeth. His was subdued strength—like being in the calm eye of the storm yet knowing that tremendous power and energy are close at hand.

When Peter denied Jesus the third time and the rooster crowed, Jesus did not say, "I told you so." He merely stared at Peter (Luke 22:61). This silent rebuke was more painful and piercing than any words would ever have been.

When Pilate tried to debate and argue and cross-examine Him, Jesus would not be baited by the man. Jesus answered the basic questions and then stood mute. The fact that Jesus could stand unshaken and not be intimidated before the powerful Roman magnate, and the fact that Jesus was in control of the conversation (rather than Pilate) absolutely "amazed" Pilate (Mark 15:5).

Many times, when in difficult or awkward situations, it is what we do *not* say that speaks the loudest. Before voicing your opinion on a matter, pause, think, evaluate, and then determine if you should speak at all.

THE SUBTLE POWER OF PERSPECTIVE

Too often people are eager to dole out punishment rather than seek restoration. Jesus was just the opposite. He made people see what the truly important issues were and how to focus on them.

When the woman was caught in adultery, the people wanted to kill her. Jesus, however, wanted the woman to change her ways and lead a more virtuous life. So, He instructed the mob to have the woman stoned by sinless people. Since there *were* no sinless people, the accusers went home humbled and the woman went away changed (John 8:11). And wasn't that the real issue here?

Similarly, Jesus' disciples pointed out to Jesus that it didn't seem fair that people redeemed early in their lives were no more saved than people who were saved later in life. To this, Jesus reminded them that when compared to eternity, life on earth isn't long no matter *when* you are saved. The *real* point is to be saved sometime—*anytime!*—before you die (Matt. 20:1–16).

Our lesson from this is that we, too, should be slow to judge and quick to restore. Reasoning, patience, forgiveness, and perspective do more to reclaim a fallen or lost soul than do punishment and anger.

THE SUBTLE POWER OF PRIVACY

Although thousands of people flocked to hear Jesus teach and preach, of equal importance was His ability to sit quietly and listen privately to the concerns of others.

When Nicodemus came at night to ask his questions and share his feelings, Jesus listened respectfully and then responded to each of the man's points (John 3:1–21). When the woman at the well needed to be admonished for having lived with six men, Jesus waited until His disciples were off on an errand. Then Jesus witnessed to the woman and led her to salvation (John 4:7–26).

Many people who are not comfortable among crowds will become open and talkative if they are approached on a one-on-one basis. Going on a coffee break together or meeting for a private lunch is a good way to say, subtly, that you care about the other person *as an individual.* It worked for Jesus and it will work for you.

THE SUBTLE POWER OF A KIND ACT

I mentioned earlier that I was amazed that my surgeon would shave my knee in preparation for my operation. Imagine how much more amazing it must have been to the disciples to have Jesus wash their feet.

Jesus was always doing humble and kind acts: He spoke complimentarily of John the Baptist (Luke 7:28); he taught the disciples how to pray (Matt. 6:9–13); he held little children on his lap (Matt. 19:14). Jesus did kind things, not for personal glory, but for the benefit of others. Even when He did a miraculous thing such as turning the water into wine at the wedding, He did so to obey His mother's request, not to earn men's praise.

A kind act can have a monumental impact on people. When Jesus went to the home of little Zacchaeus, it so honored the man, he opened his heart completely to what Jesus wanted to share with him about his need for salvation.

Have you done anything kind for anyone lately? Have you unselfishly given of your time or money or talent to help someone . . . and done so in a way that did not draw attention to yourself?

Go ahead: Commit a random act of kindness. Just be subtle about it.

SCRIPTURE VERSES TO PONDER

Just then a woman who had been subject to bleeding for twelve years came up behind him and touched the edge of his cloak. She said to herself, "If I only touch his cloak, I will be healed." Jesus turned and saw her. "Take heart, daughter," he said, "your faith has healed you." And the woman was healed from that moment.

—Matthew 9:20–22

People were also bringing babies to Jesus to have him touch them. When the disciples saw this, they rebuked them. But Jesus called the children to him and said, "Let the little children come to me, and do not hinder them, for the kingdom of God belongs to such as these. I tell you the truth, anyone who will not receive the kingdom of God like a little child will never enter it."

—Luke 18:15–17

While they were still talking about this, Jesus himself stood among them and said to them, "Peace be with you." They were startled and frightened, thinking they saw a ghost. He said to them, "Why are you troubled, and why do doubts rise in your minds? Look at my hands and my feet. . . . Touch me and see."

—Luke 24:36–39

QUESTIONS TO CONSIDER

1. During the early 1990s, a movement began to challenge people to do "random acts of kindness." How would you react if you discovered upon finishing your dinner at a restaurant that a total stranger had paid your bill? How would you feel if you came home after a hard day at work and discovered that someone had mowed your lawn or weeded your garden for you? Would you be both pleased and shocked? Would it put you in a good mood for the rest of the day? Would it give you a new perspective on people? If so, what are some "random acts of kindness" you might be able to do to help a person currently in need of Christian sympathy or charity?

2. Jesus said that when the widow gave her two mites, it was more precious to God than when wealthy people gave large sums of money that they wouldn't even miss. Similarly, do you think it pleases the Lord when we do small, humble acts of kindness to people rather than just write a check to a charitable organization? In what ways are these acts different?

3. So often Jesus used a simple touch of his hand to encourage or heal or comfort someone. Have you ever been able to encourage someone just by shaking hands or putting your arm around that person's shoulder? Has such a touch ever encouraged you? What does this teach us about the need to be close to people and to allow them to be close to us?

SUGGESTED ADDITIONAL READING

Fénelon, François. *Christian Perfection*. Minneapolis: Bethany House, 1975.

Law, William. *A Serious Call to a Devout and Holy Life*. Nashville: Upper Room Press, 1952.

Sciacca, Fran. *To Yield with All Your Soul*. Colorado Springs: NavPress, 2002.

Steere, Douglas. *On Beginning from Within*. New York: Harper and Row, 1943.

Trueblood, D. Elton. *The Humor of Christ*. New York: Harper and Row, 1964.

Yoder, John Howard. *The Politics of Jesus*. Grand Rapids: Eerdmans, 1972.

CHAPTER 23

WE CAN'T TAKE IT WITH US

My father is a self-made man. As an eighth-grade dropout, he rose to become president of three successful companies. He believes that a bit of a struggle in life isn't so bad. It builds character. And to that end, he claims that when he dies, his last will and testament will read, "Being of sound mind, I spent every dime I had while I was alive."

Now, before you begin to feel sorry for me in my sad prospects of never receiving any inheritance, let me tell you that I hope my father really carries through on his plan. I'm serious.

My father is a good Christian man. He has given hours of his time and a great deal of his money in support of orphanages, schools, churches, and worthy civic causes. The Lord, in turn, has blessed my father with financial and other rewards.

If my father, after having led a "rich" life in *all* aspects of the word, were to die penniless, he would achieve the ultimate goal of a fulfilled life. Let me explain to you why that is less paradoxical than you might believe it to be.

From the world's perspective, the attainment of money, land, and other tangible goods is the only way to determine whether or not a person has been successful in life. In fact, one famous Hollywood movie star and recording artist has a separate building next to his home that contains hundreds of toy trains, miles of railroad track, and thousands of model railroading accessories. On the door to this building is a brass plate with the engraved message, "The Guy Who Dies with the Most Toys Wins!"

From a Christian perspective, nothing could be further from the truth. Jesus taught that to spend a life hoarding material goods rather than to share with the needy was to put one's soul in an indefensible position when brought before the judgment seat of God. Thus, the guy who dies with the most of *anything* actually *loses*.

In Luke 12:15–21 Jesus told the story of a wealthy landowner whose harvests were so bountiful, his barns couldn't contain all the crops. Instead of donating the excess food to people who were less fortunate, the man ordered his little barns torn down and larger barns built. In this way, he could store all the food and keep it all to himself.

That very night the man died. His soul was called into judgment. His earthly wealth and possessions were of no value to him as he stood before God.

That story is reminiscent of a story reported in a major metropolitan newspaper in 1937, the day after John D. Rockefeller died. Rockefeller's chief accountant was approached by a newspaper reporter who asked, "Hey! Just how many millions did old J. D. leave behind?" The accountant smirked mirthlessly, then replied, "All of them."

How true, how true.

The oft-quoted catch phrase, "Ya can't take it with ya," is actually biblical in nature. It was Job who said four thousand years ago, "Naked came I out of my mother's womb, and naked shall I return thither" (Job 1:21 KJV). You would think that after all these years, we would have learned the truth of that lesson. But we haven't.

The same problem was true during Christ's time on Earth. A rich young prince came to Jesus one day and asked to be told how to obtain eternal life. Jesus told him to obey the commandments. The young man said that he was already doing that.

Then Jesus added that the prince should distribute all of his personal wealth to the poor. This saddened the prince, for he enjoyed hoarding his riches to himself.

And when Jesus saw that he was very sorrowful, he said, How
hardly shall they that have riches enter into the kingdom of
God! (Luke 18:24 KJV)

What was the lesson here? Was it that it's sinful to be financially
prosperous? No, not at all. The lesson was that there is a better defini-
tion of "rich." There is nothing wrong in being financially well-to-do,
so long as it does not make you spiritually poor.

Jesus taught that those people who make sacrifices in order to serve
God *and* serve the needy will be blessed "in this present time, and in
the world to come" (Luke 18:30 KJV). In other words, we get "the best
of both worlds," to put it in very contemporary terms.

So it is, then, that I can rejoice with my dad when he tells everyone
he plans to die penniless. He knows the secret: The guy who dies with
the *fewest* toys wins!

SCRIPTURE VERSES TO PONDER

A certain ruler asked him, "Good teacher, what must I do to
inherit eternal life?"

"Why do you call me good," Jesus answered. "No one is
good—except God alone. You know the commandments: 'Do
not commit adultery, do not murder, do not steal, do not give
false testimony, honor your father and mother.'"

"All these I have kept since I was a boy," he said.

When Jesus heard this, he said to him, "You still lack one
thing. Sell everything you have and give to the poor, and you
will have treasure in heaven. Then come, follow me."

When he heard this, he became very sad, because he was a
man of great wealth. Jesus looked at him and said, "How hard
it is for the rich to enter the kingdom of God! Indeed, it is
easier for a camel to go through the eye of a needle than for a
rich man to enter the kingdom of God."

Those who heard this asked, "Who then can be saved?"

Jesus replied, "What is impossible with men is possible with God."

—Luke 18:18–27

Command those who are rich in this present world not to be arrogant nor to put their hope in wealth, which is so uncertain, but to put their hope in God, who richly provides us with everything for our enjoyment. Command them to do good, to be rich in good deeds, and to be generous and willing to share.

—1 Timothy 6:17–18

Questions to Consider

1. British author W. Somerset Maugham once remarked, "Money is the sixth sense which makes all the other five work better." In what ways would you agree or disagree with this statement from a Christian standpoint?
2. In what ways do you think the lust for money has ruined many of the things we used to enjoy? Consider, for example, professional sports, music concerts, and television.
3. Think of people in the Bible who were wealthy, yet did good things with their wealth. (Begin with such people as Solomon, Zacchaeus, and Joseph of Arimathea.)
4. At the end of Job's trials, God doubled the amount of great wealth Job originally had. What message is this from God about wealth itself not being bad?
5. The Bible teaches that if a person does not work, neither should that person eat. In what way has man, with his gambling casinos and government lotteries, tried to go against this basic teaching of the Scriptures?
6. In the end times, no one will be able to buy or trade or sell without the "mark of the beast." How does this imply that Satan sees financial control as a key factor in world domination?

SUGGESTED ADDITIONAL READING

Bright, Bill. *A Handbook of Concepts for Living.* San Bernardino, Calif.: Here's Life Publishers, 1981.

Lockerbie, D. Bruce. *The Timeless Moment.* Westchester, Ill.: Cornerstone Books, 1980.

Smith, Hannah. *The Christian's Secret of a Happy Life.* Old Tappan, N.J.: Revell, 1968.

Tozer, A. W. *The Pursuit of God.* Harrisburg, Pa.: Christian Publications, 1948.

Wald, Oletta. *The Joy of Discovery in Bible Study.* Minneapolis: Augsburg, 1977.

Willmer, Wesley K., with Martyn Smith. *God and Your Stuff.* Colorado Springs: NavPress, 2002.

CHAPTER 24

USELESS WEALTH

One of the greatest gem collections in the world is on display at the Smithsonian Institute in Washington, DC. If you visit there, a guide will direct you to a special display that contains the Hope Diamond.

"What you see here," the guide will explain, "is the most famous gem in all of history. The Hope Diamond is the largest blue diamond ever discovered. It came from India, where it was rumored to have been the magic eye of the Hindu idol Rama Sita. When it was stolen, a curse was put on it."

The guide will pause to let this sink in, then continue. "After leaving India, the Hope Diamond became the property of Louis XVI of France and his wife, Marie Antoinette, both of whom were beheaded. Subsequently, the diamond was owned by Simon Montharides, a wealthy Greek jeweler, then by Subaya, the sweetheart of a Turkish sultan, then by Evelyn Walsh McLean, a flashy socialite, all of whom had great tragedy come into their lives."

The guide then digresses a moment to explain how East Indian diamond merchants used to weigh a gem by balancing it against the tiny seeds of the carob tree; hence, the modern term "carat weight" came into the language.

"The Hope Diamond was donated to the Smithsonian in 1958 by

Winston's Jewelers," says the guide. "It will always remain here, but if it were ever sold, the price would be $200 million."

The crowd always gasps upon hearing this figure. Someone finally asks, "But why is it worth so much? It's beautiful, yes . . . but for $200 million you could buy a warehouse full of diamonds."

The guide is prepared for this question.

"The Hope Diamond is valuable not only for its flawless beauty," he explains, "but also because it is a source of great power. A blue gem like this can function as a semiconductor of electricity because it has what scientists call an 'atomic hole' in it. Thus, it can transmit messages to satellites, space ships, or tracking stations hundreds of thousands of miles out in space. The blue diamonds are the only gems capable of this electrical transference."

The crowd nods in admiration, but the guide continues.

"Furthermore, a blue diamond can identify and register alterations or changes in delicate electrical machines. For example, in calibrating medical instruments, the Hope Diamond could register differences in temperature as small as one five-hundredth [1/500] of a degree Celsius."

Murmurs can be heard through the crowd. The guide smiles as he sees he is succeeding in verifying the value of the diamond to everyone. But, he adds even more proof.

"The Hope Diamond is chemically inert," says the guide. "As such, if a person was suffering from cancer, blue diamonds such as this one could be set around that portion of the person's body that needed to receive radiation. Because blue diamonds measure radiation as well as heat, the diamonds could designate to the therapist whether she was accurately sending the radiation to the cancer cells or inaccurately to the surrounding healthy cells."

"Amazing!" . . . "Incredible!" the listeners say in genuine astonishment.

"Oh, yes," the guide agrees. "Truly, the Hope Diamond is a miracle gem. It can transmit signals thousands of miles, it can measure heat and radiation to hundredths of a degree, it can help defeat cancer, and it can develop important industrial and medical instruments."

Everyone nods in agreement. But then a discerning child speaks up.

"Something's bothering me," the child says, scratching his head.

"Oh?" asks the guide. "And what's that?"

"Well," the little boy begins, "you say this diamond is worth $200 million because it can do so many miraculous things."

"Yes?"

"But if it just stays here in the museum every day, underneath that heavy glass plate, all locked up and secured, and it never gets put to use . . . isn't it actually worthless?"

And suddenly, both the crowd and the guide fall silent. The child, of course, is right.

Interestingly, a parallel to this museum scene is played out in homes each day. People who are in desperate situations of loneliness, fear, confusion, anxiety, stress, guilt, or grief are pacing their floors until their carpets are threadbare. They are wringing their hands, biting their lips, pulling their hair, and blotting their tears.

"Oh," they cry out, "if only there was some help for me."

And there, sitting upright on a bookshelf, right at eye level near where they are pacing, is a beautiful, leather bound, never-opened Bible. It is a show item, part of the household library. After all, "everyone owns a Bible."

Inside the Bible are comforting prayers, uplifting poems, inspiring stories of miracles, promises of God's love, lessons on life, hope for the future—absolutely *priceless* guides and insights for meeting all of life's crises.

And yet, as it sits there on the shelf only to be looked at from a distance and never to be pulled off its display and put into use, that Bible is as worthless as the Hope Diamond.

Fortunately, however, the Bible is not as inaccessible as the Hope Diamond. It doesn't cost $200 million to obtain God's Word. It has been freely given.

Knowing this, maybe each of us needs to give thought to someone we know of who is suffering from one of life's setbacks. Couldn't we provide that person with a priceless treasure: a *Bible*.

After all . . . that's where the real "Hope" is.

SCRIPTURE VERSES TO PONDER

Fix these words of mine in your hearts and minds; tie them as symbols on your hands and bind them on your foreheads. Teach them to your children, talking about them when you sit at home and when you walk along the road, when you lie down and when you get up. Write them on the doorframes of your houses and on your gates, so that your days and the days of your children may be many.

—Deuteronomy 11:18–21

And the words of the LORD are flawless,
  like silver refined in a furnace of clay,
    purified seven times.

—Psalm 12:6

Heaven and earth will pass away, but my words will never pass away.

—Matthew 24:35

Simon Peter answered him, "Lord, to whom shall we go? You have the words of eternal life. We believe and know that you are the Holy One of God."

—John 6:68–69

QUESTIONS TO CONSIDER

1. Ernest Hemingway, Marilyn Monroe, Sylvia Plath, Jim Morrison, Jimi Hendrix, Janis Joplin, Curt Kobain, and countless other famous authors, movie stars, singers, and personalities either killed themselves or died from wanton living. Each of these people had fame and incredible amounts of wealth. In the end, how did it all prove to be useless wealth? What "richness" was missing from their lives?

2. During the late 1980s an art gallery in Boston, Massachusetts was robbed of many of its priceless paintings. Although the thieves got away with the treasures, their joy in them was limited, for if they ever showed any of the famous paintings to anyone, their secret would be out and they'd be arrested. How do we, similarly, sometimes limit the wealth of God's love by being afraid to share it with others?

3. In many countries there are strict laws against printing, distributing, and reading Bibles. Nevertheless, believers will risk their lives to get possession of a Bible and then will spend secret hours studying the Holy Scriptures. How much "value" are these dear souls placing on God's Word? Conversely, when we let dust accumulate on our Bibles, how are we "discounting" the value of God's Word?

Suggested Additional Reading

Campolo, Tony. *Ideas for Social Action*. El Cajon, Calif.: Multnomah, 1988.

Hensley, Dennis E. *The Jesus Effect*. Boise: Pacific Press, 1991.

Owens, Ron with Jan McMurray. *Return to Worship*. Nashville: Broadman & Holman, 2002.

Packer, J. I. *A Quest for Godliness: The Puritan Vision of the Christian Life*. Wheaton: Crossway Books, 1990.

Watson, David. *I Believe in Evangelism*. Grand Rapids: Eerdmans, 1976.

CHAPTER 25

THE LEGEND OF THE PRIDEFUL ANTS

King David once asked, "Why do the heathen rage, and the people imagine a vain thing?" (Ps. 2:1 KJV). In contemporary language he would have said, "How can people dare to shake their fists in the face of God and proclaim themselves to be greater than He is?"

It's an age-old question. How often must God prove His superiority? Freidrick Nietzsche proclaimed, "God is dead." Nietzsche died in 1900, yet God still reigns. In 1912 the *Titanic* was called "the ship even God couldn't sink." On her maiden voyage, the *Titanic* struck an iceberg and sank to the bottom of the Atlantic Ocean, taking fifteen hundred of her twenty-two hundred passengers with her. In 1978, Jim Jones told his followers in Guyana that he was God and that they should quit reading their Bibles and just listen to him. In November of that year, all 912 people in that settlement were killed in one day.

The heathens continue to rage, but they never surpass God.

A wonderful illustration of the futility of their vainglorious efforts was given by Dr. Walter Wilson during a youth rally in 1936 at Winona Lake, Indiana. Though never published, it was told to me by an elderly gentleman who was one of the teenagers attending that 1936 rally.

It seems there was a sharp bend in the railroad line near Oletha, Kansas. The New York to San Francisco Express came across those tracks once every week. As the train took the bend at Oletha at high speed, several crumbs of food would fly out of the dining car windows and land outside near the tracks.

The ants in that area discovered these bread crumbs and started hauling them back to their ant colony a mile away. After several months of this, the head ant announced that this hauling was too much work. He ordered that a new ant hill be dug only fifty yards from the track. This proved much easier for the ants, but after three months they decided that it would be even easier if their ant hill were only twenty feet from the track. So, once again they moved.

Soon, the ants were fat and lazy. They had lots of bread crumbs and hardly any distance to have to haul them. Still, they weren't satisfied. They decided that an even better arrangement would be for them to move their ant colony between the railroad tracks and to have the stewards drop crumbs directly between the cars as the train passed overhead.

So, the head ant sent a telegram to New York, setting forth his demands. He added a threat, insisting that if the railroad company did not comply, the ants would set up a blockade and not allow the train to pass.

When no response came back from the company, the ants set to work to build their blockade. For six days they piled sand on the tracks and moved pebbles into small piles on the railroad ties. It was hard work, but they knew it would be worth it when the railroad company met their demands.

On the seventh day the ants were all assembled between the tracks amid their sand and pebble barricades. They smiled as they heard the distant train whistle and felt the ground rumble as the train approached. *Now* they'd show that train company who was in control of this situation. They began to laugh and stand on their hind legs and shake their other legs at the train in derision. My, what a grand day this was for the ants!

Ten seconds later, the New York to San Francisco Express roared through that spot at eighty miles an hour. Its heavy wheels crushed the sand on the tracks. The train's great rumbling vibrations flattened the piles of pebbles. Its blinding speed created a whirlwind that sent the ants flying through the air in every direction.

At that instant on board the train, a coal-man turned casually to the engineer and asked, "Did you feel something just then?"

"No," the engineer said, shaking his head. "Not a thing."

"Hmmm," said the coal-man, "must have been my imagination."

And, with that, the train continued to roll mightily forward.

SCRIPTURE VERSES TO PONDER

O LORD, God of our fathers, are you not the God who is in heaven? You rule over all the kingdoms of the nations. Power and might are in your hand, and no one can withstand you.

—2 Chronicles 20:6–7

Be exalted, O LORD, in your strength;
we will sing and praise your might.

—Psalm 21:13

Finally, be strong in the Lord and in his mighty power.

—Ephesians 6:10

And we pray this in order that you may live a life worthy of the Lord and may please him in every way: bearing fruit in every good work, growing in the knowledge of God, being strengthened with all power according to his glorious might so that you may have endurance and patience, and joyfully giving thanks to the Father, who has qualified you to share in the inheritance of the saints in the kingdom of light.

—Colossians 1:10–12

QUESTIONS TO CONSIDER

1. When the *Titanic* sailed its maiden voyage, the passage line billed it as "the ship even God couldn't sink." Nevertheless, one of God's icebergs ripped the ship and sank it. Can you think of other incidents from history wherein man has shaken his fist at God and has lived to regret it? What incidents from biblical history, such as the building of the Tower of Babel, can you recall which revealed the foolishness of man's efforts to mock God or be His equal?

2. God is patient and forgiving, but even God's patience has a limit. When God destroyed Sodom and Gomorrah . . . when He caused the Great Flood . . . when He closed the Red Sea on the Egyptian soldiers . . . in these and other equally awesome judgments, what do you think God was revealing about His character? What lessons about our need to be disciplined, faithful, and obedient to God can we take away from reading about such incidents?

3. Have you ever really tried to comprehend some measure of the might and power of God? Do some research on volcanoes, hurricanes, cyclones, earthquakes, tidal waves, and blizzards. These natural occurrences are stunning in their power, yet all are controlled by the God of the universe. Does this humble you? Does it remind you of the strength of the One to whom you have yielded your life and, thus, make you feel protected?

SUGGESTED ADDITIONAL READING

Bright, Bill. *Ten Basic Steps Toward Christian Maturity.* San Bernardino, Calif.: Here's Life Publishers, 1981.

Jensen, Irving Lester. *Enjoy Your Bible.* Chicago: Moody, 1969.

McDowell, Josh. *Evidence That Demands a Verdict.* San Bernardino, Calif.: Here's Life Publishers, 1979.

Mears, Henrietta. *What the Bible Is All About.* Ventura, Calif.: Regal, 1982.

Morgenthaler, Sally. *Worship Evangelism*. Grand Rapids: Zondervan, 2002.

Sterrett, T. Norton. *How to Understand Your Bible*. Downer's Grove, Ill.: InterVarsity, 1974.

CHAPTER 26

BLOOD IS THICKER THAN . . . ANYTHING

Many years ago I invited one of my coworkers to attend church with me. He declined, saying it was too morbid and bizarre.

"Morbid? Bizarre?" I said, genuinely confused. "Whatever do you mean?"

"I went to a church service not long ago and it bordered on the macabre," he explained. "Every song was about being covered with blood—that's *all* they sang about. You know, 'Are you washed in the blood of the Lamb?' and 'There is a fountain filled with blood, drawn from Immanuel's veins' and 'What can wash away my sins . . . nothing but the blood of Jesus' and on and on. It gave me the creeps."

I started to respond, but he continued rapidly.

"And then the message was more of the same," he said. "The pastor talked about the shed blood of Christ and its power of atonement. And then they held a communion service and had people drink grape juice as a symbol of blood. It was morbid, man! I never want to go through anything like that again."

Until that conversation, I had never given thought to what the gospel message must sound like to those who are out of the faith. Having grown up in a God-honoring, Bible-believing church, it had never occurred to me that our emphasis on the blood of Christ might sound shocking to nonbelievers.

On the other hand, that conversation also made me wonder if those of us who knew about the atoning blood of Christ had become so "comfortable" with it, we were no longer amazed at how great a sacrifice had been made. Maybe my friend was closer to the appropriate response to our songs and sermons than my fellow church members and I were. If we were no longer being jolted and shaken and awed by the blood sacrifice of Christ, perhaps we were becoming complacent and ungrateful. God forbid that that should happen.

Romans 5:9 tells us that "having . . . been justified by His blood, we shall be saved from the wrath of God through Him" (NASB). Unless we are covered with this blood of justification, we are doomed to eternal damnation.

Recently, I happened to be watching a television news account of the arrest and trial of a man who had been accused of viciously murdering his wife and children with a knife. Neighbors had heard screaming on the night of the murders, but they had not given it much thought until two weeks later, when it was reported on TV that the bodies of the victims had been found in shallow graves in a field outside of town. Then the neighbors called the police.

When the police entered the home of the victims, they found it to be immaculately clean. The murderer had shampooed all the carpets, washed and ironed all the curtains and drapes, and polished all the woodwork. He had cleaned every window inside and out, had polished every piece of furniture, and had even repainted all the bedrooms and hallways.

The police found no fingerprints, no blood stains, no shredded clothing, and no signs of a struggle anywhere.

The man's story was that he and his wife had had an argument a month earlier and that she had taken the kids and left him. He said he'd had no idea of where they were until he'd been told their bodies had been found.

The police officers doubted the man's story. They brought in a forensics team and sprayed the man's bedroom, bathroom, and hallway walls and floors with a chemical compound known as Luminal. This compound has the ability to permeate paint and to show up as a florescent color when it comes in contact with blood. The police waited a few moments and then, there on the walls throughout the house were bloody hand prints, smear patterns of blood, and splash droplets of blood. It was grotesque, yet absolutely convincing of the man's guilt. The soap, polish, and fresh paint had not prevented the police investigators from seeing the blood.

This is a perfect example of how we, too, will one day be "investigated" by God. We may try to hide our sins with good works and generous donations and even church attendance, but God will see through that. What He will be looking for will be the blood. Either it will be there or it won't be. If it is, we will be recognized as His own. If it isn't, we will be judged accordingly.

Shed blood, indeed, is something startling. It's not something we should be complacent about. The officers investigating the murders were shocked by it appearances on the walls. So, too, should we be continually amazed by it. Christ willingly sacrificed Himself as a blood offering for our sins: "All things are cleansed with blood, and without shedding of blood there is no forgiveness" (Hebrews 9:22 NASB).

As I explained to my friend, it isn't the blood that is grotesque, but the sin it must cleanse.

SCRIPTURE VERSES TO PONDER

Jesus said to them, "I tell you the truth, unless you eat the flesh of the Son of Man and drink his blood, you have no life in you. Whoever eats my flesh and drinks my blood has eternal life, and I will raise him up at the last day. For my flesh is real food and my blood is real drink. Whoever eats my flesh and drinks my blood remains in me, and I in him. Just as the living Father sent me and I live because of the Father, so the one who feeds on me will live because of me. This is the bread

that came down from heaven. Your forefathers ate manna and
died, but he who feeds on this bread will live forever."

—John 6:53–58

This righteousness from God comes through faith in Jesus
Christ to all who believe. There is no difference, for all have
sinned and fall short of the glory of God, and are justified
freely by his grace through the redemption that came by Christ
Jesus. God presented him as a sacrifice of atonement through
faith in his blood.

—Romans 3:22–25

He did not enter by means of the blood of goats and calves;
but he entered the Most Holy Place once for all by his own
blood.

—Hebrews 9:12

QUESTIONS TO CONSIDER

1. When the worldwide epidemic of Auto Immune Deficiency Syndrome (AIDS) became obvious to everyone in the 1990s, untainted blood was a coveted life-saving commodity. However,
   to insure that blood donated to the Red Cross and to hospitals
   and clinics truly was untainted, numerous tests had to be performed on donated blood. What lesson can be found in this
   about the impure quality of man's blood, as opposed to the
   cleansing, healing, saving purity of the blood of Christ?
2. Christ taught us to observe the communion supper as a memorial of His sacrifice on the cross and as a reminder of why He
   gave Himself for us. Do you wonder sometimes if the "ritual" of
   taking communion causes us to forget its significance? How can
   we maintain our sensitivity to the sacredness of this observance?
   How can we help our children understand its importance?
3. We began this chapter by reminding ourselves that to non-

Christians, the Bible's focus on blood atonement may seem something of a shock. In what ways have you been able to share the true meaning of blood atonement with unbelievers in a way that helps them understand its significance, yet does not shock them?

SUGGESTED ADDITIONAL READING

Chesser, Barbara Russell. *Because You Care.* Waco, Tex.: Word, 1988.

Faulkner, Paul. *Making Things Right When Things Go Wrong.* Fort Worth, Tex.: Sweet Publishing, 1986.

Walster, Elaine, and G. William. *A New Look at Love.* Reading, Mass.: Addison-Wesley, 1978.

Webber, Robert E. *Worship Is a Verb.* Peabody, Mass.: Hendrickson, 2002.

Werner, Hazen G. *The Bible and the Family.* Nashville: Abingdon, 1966.

Zimmerman, Carle C. *Family and Civilization.* New York: Harper Brothers, 1947.

CHAPTER 27

QUIT SHELLACKING THE COCOONS

Recently I was walking past observation windows of insect specimens in a large walk-through terrarium at a city zoo. Part of the exhibit featured a climate-controlled caged area that recreated a rain forest. Large-winged butterflies were allowed to fly freely. I was awestruck by their agile grace and iridescent colors.

Halfway through the rain forest walk, there was a large sheet of plywood mounted on a post. On the board, spaced six inches apart, were the chrysalises from which these various butterflies had emerged. In preparing this display, someone had shellacked the cocoons so that they would be shiny, bright, and eye-appealing. Note cards underneath the exhibits highlighted the structure, design, and functionality of each cocoon.

As I read these note cards, I had to chuckle. It occurred to me that no matter how much shellac might be sprayed on a cocoon to make it more eye-appealing, and no matter how many words of praise might be written or spoken to glorify the cocoons, no butterfly would be eager to move back inside.

After all, what would be the motivation to return to the cocoon? It was dark; it was confining; it was constricting and suppressive. Butterflies struggle vigorously to break free of such entrapments. Once loosed, they fly high and never want to look back.

How odd it is that humans are sometimes less pragmatic than a simple butterfly. As Christians, we say that we hold dearly the passages of Scripture that assure us we have been "born again" and that we are "new creatures" in Christ. Despite this, we often return to the cocoon of sin we have broken free from. In fact, we may even be guilty of spraying shellac on that cocoon, thinking we are serving God in the process.

Let me explain what I mean by that.

I have heard individuals stand in congregational meetings and share a testimony that includes fifteen minutes of chronicling that person's past sins. Each wayward deed of an unregenerate life is passionately extolled, often in graphic detail. The logic for doing this seems to be for the convert to emphasize the power Christ had to redeem one who was lost in vile sin. The irony, however, is that, as the person is confessing innumerable transgressions, God has no knowledge of what is being talked about. He has not only *forgiven* those sins, He has *forgotten* them.

If God does not look back on our cocoon of sin, why should we waste time shellacking it?

In no way do I wish to discount the grace by which Christ redeems lost sinners . . . surely myself included. Even the apostle Paul felt compelled to admit publicly the magnitude of his former sins before being confronted by the Lord (1 Tim. 1:15). However, Paul chose to focus his preaching and teaching primarily on Jesus, not on himself. When Paul said, "By the grace of God I am what I am" (1 Cor. 15:10), he was saying that, yes, Christ had redeemed him, but He did so for the purpose of serving the Lord as a vibrant, forward-thinking, walking witness of what a new life in Christ was all about (Acts 13:47).

Paul shared the good news of salvation with everyone, whether a common jailer or a Roman ruler. We should do likewise. The Bible warns us that a pig, even after being washed clean, will return to wallow in a mud hole (2 Peter 2:22); yet a butterfly, once free of the dark cocoon, never returns.

If we wish to draw others to Christ, we need to be like the butterflies. We should separate ourselves from our past cocoons of sin, both physically and emotionally. Rather than dredge up past wrongs, we should focus on current blessings (Deut. 28:3, 6). Rather than remember our previous days of shame, we should press heavenward to our future days of glory (Phil. 3:14).

Butterflies, though gorgeous, live very brief lives. Some live a few months, others merely a couple of days. During that life span, however, they are always objects of beauty. Similarly, our lives as Christians are "but a vapor." This should behoove us to use our precious time to reflect the beauty of Christ.

However, we cannot spread our wings if we are still stuck in the cocoon.

SCRIPTURE VERSES TO PONDER

For as high as the heavens are above the earth,
    so great is his love for those who fear him;
as far as the east is from the west,
    so far has he removed our transgressions from us.

—Psalm 103:11–12

O LORD, truly I am your servant;
I am your servant, the son of your maidservant;
    you have freed me from my chains.

—Psalm 116:16

Forget the former things;
    do not dwell on the past.
See, I am doing a new thing!
    Now it springs up; do you not perceive it?
I am making a way in the desert
    and streams in the wasteland.

—Isaiah 43:18–19

If the Son sets you free, you will be free indeed.

—John 8:36

QUESTIONS TO CONSIDER

1. Christ has promised us that we become new creations upon accepting Him as Savior. Although we can accept this emotionally, why does it still seem hard for us to comprehend mentally?
2. Is it possible for a person, even when publicly denouncing his or her former sins, to be evidencing an aspect of pride?
3. A furry, ugly caterpillar can be transformed into a lovely butterfly. In what other way does God use nature as a metaphor of the transforming power of His grace?
4. Why is it spiritually healthy to shed the cocoons of our past sins as we endeavor to go forward in service to Christ?

SUGGESTED ADDITIONAL READING

Barna, George and Mark Hatch. *Boiling Point*. Ventura, Calif.: Regal, 2001.

Brin, David. *The Transparent Society*. Reading, Mass.: Addison-Wesley, 1998.

Colson, Charles, and Nancy Pearcey. *How Now Shall We Live?* Wheaton, Ill.: Tyndale House, 1999.

Whitehead, John W. *Grasping for the Wind*. Grand Rapids: Zondervan, 2001.

CHAPTER 28

APPEARANCES SHOULDN'T BE DECEIVING

There's an old saying that warns, "You can't tell a book by its cover." That's especially true in the business of publishing.

Once, I was the guest on a television talk show where I had been asked to discuss my latest novel. The novel was not actually due to arrive in bookstores for another month yet, but advance publicity was already well underway.

The host had placed a copy of my book on a table between us so that the viewing audience could see its cover as we talked. Suddenly, the host snatched up the book and said, "Well, instead of having you *tell* us about the book, why don't I just open it at random and read a few passages to the audience?"

To his shock (for this was a live broadcast), the host then discovered that all of the pages were blank. The book was just a mock-up that had been sent to the television station by the publisher. It was for publicity purposes only. The *real* book wouldn't be on the market until the following month.

I hastily explained things to the audience, but the talk show host was so flabbergasted, he could barely finish the interview.

A few weeks later, once the real books arrived, I started to throw away the mock-up copy, but my daughter asked if she could have it. When I asked her why, she said she planned to use it as a diary. She explained that if she used a book marked "Diary," someone might sneak a peak in it and discover her intimate secrets. However, if people thought it was just one of Dad's novels, no one would pull it off the shelf. Her privacy would be guaranteed. (Hmmmmm . . .)

THE GREAT COVERUP

Like books, people aren't always consistent inwardly with what their appearance indicates outwardly. For example, during recent decades certain evangelists have been caught in worldly situations inconsistent with a Spirit-filled life. The newspaper coverage of these events has made it seem as though nothing like this has ever happened before. For a fact, the problem has existed for ages.

Jesus was confronted by the Jewish holy men. They denounced His preaching, healing, and claim to divinity. To them, Jesus responded, "Woe unto you, scribes and Pharisees, hypocrites! for ye are like unto whited sepulchres, which indeed appear beautiful outward, but are within full of dead men's bones, and of all uncleanness" (Matt. 23:27 KJV).

Like the mock-up book, the Pharisees looked perfect from the outside. Their "covers" were attractive. Inside, however, they were void, characterless, dead. Jesus called them frauds. They might have fooled other people, but not Him. Jesus flipped open the pages of their lives and exposed their blank souls.

Similarly, the apostle Paul was brought in judgment before these same Pharisees and their counterparts, the Sanhedrin. When Paul refused to recant his teachings about Christ being the true Messiah, he was hit in the face.

Paul looked at the Jewish priest and called him a "whited wall" (Acts 23:3 KJV). By this he meant that, just as rotted timber and crumbling mortar can seem to be in good shape if they are given a fresh coat of paint, so, too, did the Jewish priest seem righteous despite his decaying spirituality.

As Christians, I believe our effectiveness as witnesses would be much greater if we would concentrate on developing what is inside of us rather than always seem to be worrying about how our outward image appears.

When I was a teenager, I attended First Baptist Church of Bay City, Michigan. When the church building reached one hundred years old, it was decided that it probably wasn't safe to use any longer. The congregation voted to knock down the building and construct a new church.

When the wrecking crews came, they swung a great iron ball time and again into the church walls and steeple, but the old church would not topple. Finally, some construction workers went up into the bell tower to investigate. They came down and announced that huge timbers, two feet thick, had been inserted between the double walls of brick and mortar to provide greater stability.

"This old church is built like a castle," announced the crew boss. "The only way to bring it down will be to dismantle it. It's so solidly fortified, it could have stood *another hundred years.* You folks really underestimated the internal stamina some of these old structures have."

I've known senior saints who are like that building. They may be upward in years and appear frail on the outside, but, in truth, they are still wearing the full armor of God. More importantly, their internal souls are firm in the faith and their testimonies are strong in the Spirit of the Lord.

The lesson here is that things aren't always as they appear to be. Something attractive might just be "whitewashed." Something outwardly aged might actually be inwardly youthful. To God, however, nothing is hidden. He is the "discerner of the thoughts and intents of the heart" (Heb. 4:12 KJV). He sees things as they are. To that end, we would be wise to walk our talk, and talk our walk.

SCRIPTURE VERSES TO PONDER

Stop judging by mere appearances, and make a right judgment.
—John 7:24

As for those who seemed to be important—whatever they were makes no difference to me; God does not judge by external appearance.
—Galatians 2:6

Remember your leaders, who spoke the word of God to you. Consider the outcome of their way of life and imitate their faith.
—Hebrews 13:7

To the angel of the church in Sardis write: These are the words of him who holds the seven spirits of God and the seven stars. I know your deeds; you have a reputation of being alive, but you are dead. Wake up! Strengthen what remains and is about to die, for I have not found your deeds complete in the sight of my God. Remember, therefore, what you have received and heard; obey it, and repent. But if you do not wake up, I will come like a thief, and you will not know at what time I will come to you.
—Revelation 3:1–3

QUESTIONS TO CONSIDER

1. It has been said that "you can't tell a book by its cover." How are people often this same way?
2. If God looks upon the heart of an individual, what lesson should we draw from this regarding how we should interact with other people?
3. When the rich young ruler approached Jesus, he went away sad despite all his wealth. Why was this so?

4. When Job was being assaulted by Satan, it was his internal faith that sustained him during the loss of all his worldly goods. How was this in sharp contrast to people who lost all of their money during the Stock Market crash of 1929 or people who lost their businesses due to the assault on New York's Twin Towers on September 11, 2001?

5. It can be argued that beauty is only skin deep. Can the same be said of the spiritual depth of some people?

SUGGESTED ADDITIONAL READING

Bridges, Jenny. *I Exalt You, O God.* Colorado Springs: WaterBrook, 2001.

Cape, David, and Tommy Tenney. *God's Secret to Greatness.* Ventura, Calif.: Regal, 2001.

Cymbala, Jim, and Dean Merrill. *Fresh Power.* Grand Rapids: Zondervan, 2001.

Owens, Daniel. *In God We Trust.* Wheaton, Ill.: Crossway Books, 2001.

Rutland, Mark. *God of the Valleys.* New York: Vine, 2001.

Trent, John. *Be There!* Colorado Springs: WaterBrook, 2001.

CHAPTER 29

MAKING THE RIGHT CONNECTIONS IN LIFE

Years ago, when my daughter Jeanette was just learning her numbers, I found I could keep her occupied and quiet for hours by giving her coloring books with dot-to-dot pages in them.

"What is *this* picture?" she'd ask, holding up a page of random dots.

"I don't know," I'd admit. "You'll have to connect all the dots in the right order before we'll be able to see the finished picture. Can you do it?"

She would smile, nod, then grab a crayon and begin to slowly, painstakingly draw lines from one dot to the next. At first, she had some problems: Sometimes the numbers would run higher than she could count; other times, she'd confuse twelve with twenty-one and would connect the dots out of order; and once, she used a green crayon to create a picture of a dog that would have been better in brown or black.

I recall seeing some very bizarre dot connections in those first couple of books she worked on—buildings that resembled snowmen, cars that looked like caterpillars, and one particular airplane that came out like a hot dog in a lopsided bun.

To help Jeanette see where she had gone wrong (yet not discourage her), I would pull her onto my lap, put my big hand around her little hand, and then, moving together, we would retrace the dots in the right sequence. When the building or car or airplane then came out looking the way it should, Jeanette felt she'd had "a hand" in doing it right.

As my daughter grew older, we continued to work together on dot-to-dot puzzles; these puzzles, however, were from the book of life rather than from a coloring book. For example, sometimes Jeanette would make poor decisions about television shows she would watch or she'd disappoint friends in some way or she'd forget to do her homework.

Each of these "misconnections" would distort the picture of what Jeanette was supposed to be like. We would have to backtrack to where the wrong connection had been made and decide what the correct connection should have been. (Today, she is a professional school teacher, and I'm very pleased with how her picture has turned out.)

If I have been wise in helping my daughter learn how to "connect" her life properly, it is only because my heavenly Father has set the example for me. I, too, have made many poor connections in my life that have altered and distorted the perfect picture Christ would have me to be. In many instances, He has put His big hand around my little hand and helped me to retrace the connections the correct way.

Sometimes the Lord helps me retrace my life by sending another Christian to counsel or admonish me. For instance, many years ago I was attending graduate school and working two jobs. Sunday morning was the only day I could sleep late, so I missed Sunday school for about a month. Then one day my wife gently said, "You're my husband, Dennis. You're supposed to set an example for me." She was right. I've never missed a Sunday school class since then except for extreme illness.

Other times, the Lord helps me correct misconnections by exposing me to specific passages of Scripture. One time a Christian business associate of mine and I were trying to land a contract to provide some specialized training for a large company. The man we met with was an abrasive, foul-mouthed, coarse individual.

After enduring this man's off-color remarks for half an hour, my friend told him that we found his language offensive. My friend asked if the man would refrain from swearing while we talked. The man promptly showed us to the door and we lost the account.

Although I said nothing to my friend about his decision to speak up, I secretly wished that he would have waited until *after* we had signed the contracts. That night, however, I was preparing a devotional and, inadvertently, I came across these verses: "Be not thou envious against evil men, neither desire to be with them. For their heart studieth destruction, and their lips talk of mischief" (Prov. 24:1–2 KJV). I realized instantly that my friend had done the wise thing in separating us from that man and his company. A week later we were hired by a much more prestigious firm that offered us an even better contract.

The Lord uses many other ways to help me connect the dots of my life in proper sequence. Sometimes it's through a sermon or a hymn or a Bible commentary or an article in a Christian periodical. Other times it's through a Christian book, a film, someone's testimony, or just a quiet time of prayer and meditation. Whatever the way, He lets me know when I've used the wrong crayon or read the dot numbers backward.

And He lets me have "a hand" in making better connections.

SCRIPTURE VERSES TO PONDER

In your unfailing love you will lead
   the people you have redeemed.
In your strength you will guide them
   to your holy dwelling.

—Exodus 15:13

He makes me lie down in green pastures,
   he leads me beside quiet waters.

—Psalm 23:2

See if there is any offensive way in me,
and lead me in the way everlasting.

—Psalm 139:24

He who heeds discipline shows the way to life,
but whoever ignores correction leads others astray.

—Proverbs 10:17

Train a child in the way he should go,
and when he is old he will not turn from it.

—Proverbs 22:6

QUESTIONS TO CONSIDER

1. In what ways do many people of the twenty-first century believe they are making the right connections, only to discover later that they are forming no lasting "links" in life?
2. At what times in your life have you felt "disconnected" from Christ? What steps did you take to "reconnect" with the Lord?
3. It has been said, "It isn't what you know that gets you ahead in life, it's *who* you know." In light of biblical teachings, what would your thoughts be on this statement?
4. What actions can we take on a daily basis to assume that we will stay connected to God?
5. When was the last time you invited God to put His guarding hand around you in helping you make the right connections in life?

SUGGESTED ADDITIONAL READING

Barna, George. *Generation Next.* Ventura, Calif.: Regal, 1998.
Farrar, Steve. *Family Survival in the American Jungle.* Portland, Ore.: Multnomah, 1991.

Gallup, George, Jr., and Timothy Jones. *The Next American Spirituality: Finding God in the Twenty-First Century.* Colorado Springs: Victor Books, 2000.

Phillips, Tom. *Revival Signs: Join the New Spiritual Awakening.* Gresham, Ore.: Vision House, 1995.

Sine, Tom. *Mustard Seed Versus McWorld: Reinventing Life and Faith for the Future.* Grand Rapids: Baker, 1999.

CHAPTER 30

THE ROAD SIGNS OF LIFE

These signs . . . are not . . . for laughs alone. . . . The
face they save . . . may be your own. . . . Burma Shave

When I was a kid, there weren't a lot of big interstate highways the way there are today. Families drove the back roads in a car that traveled less than fifty miles an hour. One company that tailored its advertising to this mode of travel was the Burma-Vita Corporation, makers of Burma Shave shaving cream and aftershave lotion.

As the family car would "zip" along at forty-five miles per hour, a series of six signs would come into view, spaced one hundred paces apart. When combined, the words formed a limerick or funny saying that would make the readers laugh (as well as remind them to buy Burma Shave products). For example, you might see, "The answer to . . . a maiden's prayer . . . is *not* a chin . . . of stubby hair. . . . Burma Shave!" Or perhaps, "His face was smooth . . . and cool as ice . . . and, oh, Louise! . . . he smelled . . . so nice. . . . Burma Shave."

My brother and sister and I used to argue over whose turn it was to read the next set of Burma Shave signs. My personal favorite was, "The Bearded Lady . . . tried a jar . . . and now she is . . . a movie star. . . . Burma Shave." My mother's favorite was, "If you should think . . . she

150

likes those bristles . . . you try kissin' . . . a flower . . . with thistles. . . . Burma Shave." Dad liked, "Dewhiskered . . . kisses . . . defrost . . . the Mrs. . . . Burma Shave."

Sometimes the signs carried advice and warnings, such as, "Slow down, Pa . . . sakes alive . . . Ma just missed . . . signs four and five . . . Burma Shave" and "Our blackened forest . . . smoulders yet . . . because he flipped . . . a cigarette. . . . Burma Shave."

The first Burma Shave signs appeared in 1927 on route 65 from Minneapolis to Red Wing, Minnesota. They were installed by the company's Ph.D.s (post hole diggers). The signs were incredibly successful and, so, were spread nationwide. Even during the Great Depression, the Burma-Vita Company grossed nearly $3 million a year. However, by 1963, cars were traveling at seventy miles per hour on freeways, and if a driver craned his neck to read the signs, it might have proven fatal. So, the last Burma Shave sign went up: "All these years . . . we've done our part . . . to make your face . . . a work . . . of art. . . . Burma Shave."

Now, some forty years since those signs have disappeared, I still recall many of those words of "wits-dom." And this is ironic in a sense, because I hold four university degrees and am considered a very educated man, yet I remember the Burma Shave jingles better than I do many of the major philosophical statements I've read by Socrates, Plato, Aristotle, Descartes, Kant, and other great thinkers. The explanation of this can probably be found in Thoreau's famous line in *Walden*, "Simplify, simplify, simplify!"

I'm convinced that simplicity was the secret of the evangelistic success of the ministry of Jesus. If you think about it, His entire message was summarized in two words: "Follow me" (Matt. 4:19).

Christ gave us simple words of wisdom that were meant to encourage, as well as guide us. Consider some of these sayings that you are already familiar with:

No man can serve two masters (Matthew 6:24 KJV).

Judge not, that ye be not judged (Matthew 7:1 KJV).

Have faith in God (Mark 11:22 KJV).

A good tree bringeth . . . forth [good] fruit. . . . A good man out of the good treasure of his heart bringeth forth that which is good (Luke 6:43, 45 KJV).

He that loveth his life shall lose it; and he that hateth his life in this world shall keep it unto life eternal (John 12:25 KJV).

Though expressed in simple ways, the messages of Jesus were profound, deep, wise, and stimulating. A simple statement, such as, *a wise man builds his house upon a rock* (see Luke 6:48), carries many lessons about life. Readers know that a home built on sand will wash away during a big storm. Similarly, a "house" (be it a family, a career, or a spiritual relationship with God) will also "wash away" if there is no bedrock for a foundation. The lesson here is easy to understand, it is memorable, and it is accurate. It succeeds, not in spite of its simplicity but because of it.

I believe there are two lessons we can draw from the way Christ taught. First, if we want to be wise, we should spend time reading the Scriptures. God has given us the Bible. It is filled with the Old Testament revelations about the coming Messiah and the New Testament sermons, stories and lessons taught by that Messiah. They are expressed in simple, easy-to-follow ways. Jesus used parables, anecdotes, examples, and familiar expressions to teach us the weighty and profound matters of the ways of God. That which seemed complicated and abstruse was made understandable and clear.

A second lesson is that we should use a similar approach in witnessing when we share the gospel with others. Just as a newborn baby can only handle a diet of milk, so, too, prospective Christians must be "nursed" along in easy ways (see 1 Peter 2:2). It is far better to talk about how "God is love" (1 John 4:16) than to become involved in a deep theological debate over the causes of original sin or a discernment related to prophesy. Those are the meat and potato subjects that can be digested at later maturity.

As representatives of Christ, we can put His words of wisdom before people the same way the post hole diggers did the Burma Shave signs of old. The signs of life that Jesus gave, however, won't be limited in time the way the Burma Shave signs were. His words are valid for eternity. They are profound in meaning, yet simple in delivery.

Solomon, the wisest man who ever lived, praised the use of simple language that could be beneficial to all: "All the words of my mouth are in righteousness. . . . They are all plain to him that understandeth, and right to them that find knowledge" (Prov. 8:8–9 KJV).

That's our challenge. We need to read the simple truth Christ gave us, then share it in equally simple ways with others. So . . . "study your Bible . . . all your days . . . then share it . . . with others . . . in simple ways. . . . Burma Shave."

SCRIPTURE VERSES TO PONDER

The Levites . . . instructed the people in the Law while the people were standing there. They read from the Book of the Law of God, making it clear and giving the meaning so that the people could understand what was being read.

—Nehemiah 8:7–8

Your word is a lamp to my feet
and a light for my path. . . .
The unfolding of your words gives light;
it gives understanding to the simple.

—Psalm 119:105, 130

But as for you, continue in what you have learned and have become convinced of, because you know those from whom you learned it, and how from infancy you have known the holy Scriptures, which are able to make you wise for salvation through faith in Christ Jesus.

—2 Timothy 3:14–15

Preach the Word; be prepared in season and out of season;
correct, rebuke and encourage—with great patience and careful instruction.

—2 Timothy 4:2

QUESTIONS TO CONSIDER

1. What are some of your favorite Bible verses? How have they
   served as road signs for your life?
2. Like speeding drivers who could not read Burma Shave signs,
   how do we sometimes fail to read and learn from the Word of
   God because of our fast-paced lives?
3. In what way can we serve as God's "road signs" to others?
4. Why do you think Jesus simplified His lessons by using parables
   and stories and illustrations taken from everyday life in order
   to explain the message of salvation?
5. If someone asked you to show him or her the "road to salvation," how would you lay out the trip?

SUGGESTED ADDITIONAL READING

Barnes, M. Craig. *Sacred Thirst.* Grand Rapids: Zondervan, 2001.
Drew, Charles. *A Public Faith.* Colorado Springs: NavPress, 2001.
Fehlauer, Mike. *Life Without Fear.* Lake May, Fla.: Creation House, 2001.
Garlow, James L. *How God Saved Civilization.* Ventura, Calif.: Regal,
   2001.
Manning, Brennan. *Ruthless Trust.* San Francisco: Harper-Collins, 2001.
Vines, Jerry. *Spirit Fruit: The Graces of a Spirit-Filled Life.* Nashville:
   Broadman & Holman, 2001.

CHAPTER 31

DRESSING THE INWARD PERSON

Years ago a very successful female attorney, a member of our church, was killed in an automobile accident. This woman had always been admired for her polished, professional, even classy image. Her ladies' business outfits and dresses were hand-tailored; her shoes were modern and stylish; and her handbags, jewelry, and other accessories were very becoming.

Two months after this woman's funeral, her husband asked our pastor's wife to go through the woman's wardrobe and give her beautiful clothes to ladies in our church who were the same size. Four women benefited from this: our associate pastor's wife, our church pianist, and two ladies who sang each week in our choir.

Soon thereafter, the gorgeous clothes of the deceased lady began to appear in our church again, this time worn by other women. The outfits were easily recognizable as those that had belonged to the late attorney. As such, her "presence" seemed to still be in our midst each week.

Eventually, the clothes—pretty though they were—became less stylish as trends began to change. They also began to wear with age. In time, none of the outfits were seen any longer at our church.

I drew a lesson from that. Outward trappings are temporary, at best. No matter how well sewn and chic and fashionable a garment may be, its durability is only seasonable. Inward vestments, however, have a genuine endurance. What we "put on" internally will not become frayed or dated.

David proclaimed, "Thy word have I hid in mine heart, that I might not sin against thee" (Ps. 119:11 KJV). His heart was adorned with Scripture verses, engraved where they could not erode or be marred. Similarly, Paul encouraged his fellow Christians to "put on a heart of compassion, kindness, humility, gentleness and patience" (Col. 3:12 NASB). These holy raiments will drape the heart in everlasting beauty.

Isaiah wrote, "Thou wilt keep him in perfect peace, whose mind is stayed on thee" (Isa. 26:3 KJV). Isaiah's mind was draped in peace and contentment because it was constantly thinking about the protective love of God. This serene mental setting was always arrayed in tranquility, for God never abandons His children.

Jeremiah proclaimed that anyone who loves and reveres God shall have a "soul [that] shall be as a watered garden" (Jer. 31:12 KJV). Just as a lovely garden is adorned with multicolored flowers and luscious fruits and vegetables, so too is the soul of a righteous person. This verdant soul, however, does not have an autumn during which it loses its loveliness and abundance. Instead, it blooms eternal and is always in season.

Solomon stated that the marrow of our bones should be arrayed with the respect of the Lord (Prov. 3:7–8). He also stated that a tongue arrayed in wholesomeness is like a tree of life (Prov. 15:4). Job said our entire being should be decked out in the "majesty and excellency" of God's benevolence (Job 40:10 KJV).

So it is, then, that we see that external arrayment loses its appeal and usefulness in a very short time. However, the inward arrayment, when made of righteous elements, will keep the heart, mind, soul, tongue, and bones adorned in such majestic clothing, they will never be out of vogue.

SCRIPTURE VERSES TO PONDER

But the LORD said to Samuel, "Do not consider his appearance or his height, for I have rejected him. The LORD does not look at the things man looks at. Man looks at the outward appearance, but the LORD looks at the heart."

—1 Samuel 16:7

Do not store up for yourselves treasures on earth, where moth and rust destroy, and where thieves break in and steal. But store up for yourselves treasures in heaven, where moth and rust do not destroy, and where thieves do not break in and steal. For where your treasure is, there your heart will be also.

—Matthew 6:19–21

You are all sons of God through faith in Christ Jesus, for all of you who were baptized into Christ have clothed yourselves with Christ.

—Galatians 3:26–27

QUESTIONS TO CONSIDER

1. It has been said that "clothes make the man." How does this statement run counter to Christ's teachings?
2. When Princess Diana died, her dresses were put up at auction and brought tens of thousands of dollars. What message does this send to people who knew this woman well?
3. Jesus did not dress in fine clothes, yet what happened when the sick woman touched the hem of his garment? Why?
4. For more than twenty years a famous designer known as Blackwell announced his annual list of "The Ten Worst Dressed Women." The list was published in all of the major newspapers. Why would such a list be "big news"? What does it say about the culture we now live in?

SUGGESTED ADDITIONAL READING

Hersh, Sharon A. *Brave Hearts.* Colorado Springs: WaterBrook, 2001.

Lutzer, Erwin W. *Ten Lies About God.* El Paso: Word, 2001.

Nelson, Alan, and Gene Appel. *How to Change Your Church.* El Paso: Word, 2001.

Ryken, Philip Graham. *When You Pray.* Wheaton: Crossway Books, 2001.

Wilkinson, Bruce. *The Prayer of Jabez.* Portland, Ore.: Multnomah, 2000.

About the Author

Dr. Dennis E. Hensley is the author of more than forty books, including such titles as *Man to Man: Becoming the Believer God Called You to Be* (Kregel), *Surprises and Miracles of the Season* (Beacon Hill), *Teach Yourself Grammar and Style* (Macmillan), *How to Write What You Love and Make a Living at It* (Random House), and *The Jesus Effect* (Pacific Press). Six of his books have been novels. He has also written more than 150 short stories and 3000 newspaper and magazine articles.

Dr. Hensley holds four university degrees in communications, including a Ph.D. in English from Ball State University where he was named "Distinguished Doctoral Graduate in English." He has received numerous other honors, including the "Dorothy Hamilton Memorial Writing Award," the "Indiana University Award for Teaching Excellence," and a "City of Fort Wayne Bicentennial Gold Medallion." During the 2000–2001 academic year he filled the chair as "Distinguished Visiting Professor of English and Journalism" at the graduate communication arts school of Regent University in Virginia Beach, Virginia. Currently, he is a professor of English at Taylor University's Fort Wayne campus, where he is director of the professional writing major.

Dr. Hensley and his wife, Rose, have two grown children, Nathan and Jeanette. From 1970–1971, Dr. Hensley served as a sergeant in the U.S. Army and was awarded six medals for service in Vietnam. He has been a guest speaker at more than 100 writer's conferences worldwide.